Efsli 2013

Conference Proceedings

13th – 15th September 2013

Ljubljana, Slovenia

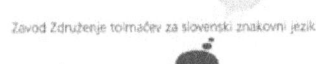

ISBN: 9789081306577
© European Forum of Sign Language Interpreters, 2014

Edited by: Darja Fišer, Jolanda Peverelli

Graphic & Design: Jolanda Peverelli, Darja Fišer

Cover photos: Slobodan Simić

Printed by: Publish-X, Createspace

All rights reserved
No part of this publication may be produced, stored in a retrieval system or transmitted in any form or any means (electronic, photocopying, recording or otherwise), without the prior written permission of the publisher.

This publication is made possible with support of the EU Erasmus + Programme

The information and views set out in this publication are those of the author(s) and do not necessarily reflect the official opinion of the European Union. Neither the European Union institutions and bodies nor any person acting on their behalf may be held responsible for the use which may be made of the information contained therein.

Table of contents

Foreword by the efsli President 4

Jasna Bauman (Slovenia): Calling centre for people with hearing impairment 5

Hilde Haualand (Norway): Interpreting ideals and relaying rights 12

Peter Llewellyn-Jones (UK): The impact of monological interpreting models approaches when applied to remote interpretations 23

Knut Weinmeister and Lea Schramm (Germany): The signing questions and answer tool sqat – a tool for translation from written language into sign language and vice versa 51

Roger Beeson, David Wolfenden, Mo Bergson and Christopher Stone (UK): Modern technology and modern interpreter 66

Mark Zaurov (Germany): Online interpreting: the advantages of new technologies supporting the needs of interpreters and their customers 72

Nicole Montagna (USA): The digital revolution and sign language interpreting, impact and implications 75

Helen Fuller and Brigitte Francois (UK): Technology vs interpreter-support or replacement? 77

Okan Kubus (Germany): Advantages and challenges of video relay sevices (VRS) in Germany: perspectives of vrc interpreters and deaf customers 84

Tracey Tyler (UK): Don't leave me hanging on the telephone… 87

efsli 2013 proceedings

Foreword by the efsli President
Peter Llewellyn-Jones

The theme of the 2013 efsli conference, "TECHNOLOGY vs. INTERPRETER: support or replacement?" (hosted by the Slovenian Association of Sign Language Interpreters) was particularly timely because we have seen a proliferation of web-based 'remote' interpreting services over the past (very few) years. Just as it can be argued that the invention of the telephone led to Deaf people being seriously disadvantaged in many areas of life, it is equally true that the development of the internet and live video-streaming technology has the potential for levelling the playing field and allowing Deaf people, perhaps for the first time, to access information and communicate as easily as hearing people can when they pick up a phone. What is still be needed, though, is the interface that allows signed language using Deaf people to interact with those who communicate through the medium of speech and that interface, in its human form, is the interpreter.

Just as machine translation will need many more incarnations before it can begin to replace the human translator, technology still has a long way to go before it can do away with human interpreters. The question we are left with is this; if the modern world has had to adapt as technology has developed, in what ways does the interpreter need to adapt so that Deaf people can make the most of the video technology now available?

This and many other questions are discussed in the papers that follow. There are reports of successful services being established for specific purposes and communities, and questions raised about the traditional 'roles' and approaches of interpreters and whether they are adequate or appropriate for the new environments in which they now work.

The papers in this volume won't answer all of those questions but they are an excellent starting point for the discussions and debates that are likely to dominate our field for some time to come.

Jasna Bauman (Slovenia): Calling centre for people with hearing impairment

Jasna Bauman is a qualified Social Worker with over 30 years experience of working with Deaf people and is also a Certified Slovenian Sign Language interpreter. She participated in the working group appointed by the Minister of Labour, Family and Social Affairs to establish the legal recognition of Deaf people's right to interpretation, and was responsible for the design and adoption of the knowledge and skills criteria necessary for certification as a Slovenian Sign Language Interpreter. She is also a member of the Examination Board for the Certification and State Licensing of intetrpreters. She co-wrote the project 'Call center for people with hearing impairment' and is a member of the Government Council for Slovenian Sign Language. She is an author and organiser of annual conferences dedicated to the issues of Deaf peoples' right to an interpreter, and the standardising of Slovenian Sign Language. In 2009 she was chief 'editor of expertise' of 'The Status of the Slovenian Sign Language'. She has participated in various professional meetings and international conferences and is the author of a range of professional articles. In 2002 she was the Project Coordinator of 'The Practical Multimedia Dictionary of Slovenian Sign Language', for which she received the European Language Merit Award. Since 2004, she had been the Director of the Institute and Association of Slovenian Sign Language.

Contact details for correspondence: jasna.zdruzenje @ t-2.net

Abstract: In the past, deaf people have too often been dependent on the goodwill of their relatives, random acquaintances and friends when they needed to establish communication to access information or services provided by public institutions. The development of technology has made it possible for hearing impaired people to have 24-hour access to this information and with it contributed to their independent living. In 2009 we began to implement an experimental project - the Call center for people with hearing impairment - the purpose of which was to establish a means of communication for the deaf user, via Slovenian Sign Language Interpreters, so that they can acquire information relevant to their lives and their work. To this end, we have developed a computer application through which deaf people access a call center through all available means of communication and obtain a variety of information through its staff of interpreters. In the paper we demonstrate the work of a call center for people with hearing impairment, its methods of operation and the results of a survey that was conducted among its users.

Relay centre for persons with hearing impairment

Introduction

The Equality of Opportunities for Persons with Disabilities Act, adopted by the National Assembly of the Republic of Slovenia in 2010, stipulated the establishment of a Relay centre for persons with hearing impairment. By adopting this provision, the Government of the Republic of Slovenia pursued the Convention on rights of the handicapped to make the necessary adjustments to enable them to access information. On the basis of this Act the Relay centre for people with hearing impairment was established in 2009 within the framework of the Association of Slovenian Sign Language Interpreters. The establishment of the Relay centre is also in response to numerous appeals by the deaf and hearing-impaired community regarding their previous inability to acquire information from, and in the field of, government authorities, local government bodies, public authorities and providers of public services. The paper presents a detailed description of the Relay centre.

The goals of the relay centre for persons with hearing disabilities

Due to loss of hearing, the deaf and hearing impaired are not able to use the universal communication channels available to people without a hearing disability. To give a couple of examples: they cannot make a phone call to their GP and schedule an appointment; they cannot call the Administrative unit and ask about the opening hours at the job centre, etc. These are just two everyday situations which hearing people can tackle without difficulty because communication with these entities is tailored for the majority, hearing population. Deaf and persons with hearing impairments were disadvantaged and had to rely on the goodwill of their family members, neighbours and friends who they had to ask to make the necessary phone call on their behalf. In order to enable the deaf and hearing-impaired to establish communication with institutions and access the required information in a a way that met their requirements, we set up the Relay centre for persons with hearing impairment, symbolising a way towards independence, empowerment and independent life for the deaf and hearing-impaired community.

How does the relay centre for persons with hearing impairment work?

The needs of the users were the prime consideration when establishing the Relay centre. The technical solutions were chosen from the available communication means used by the deaf and hearing-impaired, while our guiding principle was to facilitate the use of the relay centre with communication tools the users were already familiar with and didn't require any additional adjustments. We also did not want the use of the centre to cause additional expenses for the future users. In order to integrate all the communication means already used by the deaf and hearing-impaired, we designed a computer application available online at kc.tolmaci.si. The relay centre facilitates communication of the deaf and hearing-impaired, by acquiring the needed information on their behalf and forwarding the information back to the user. The form of communication is chosen by the user and enables the users to use the form he or she is most familiar with. The Relay centre users can communicate with the relay centre in the following ways:

- By sending an SMS
- By making a video phone relay with a UMTS (smart) phone,
- By making a video phone relay call on their computer,
- By sending an e-mail,
- By having a live on-line conversation (chat),
- By sending a fax.

The Relay centre is open 24 hours a day, every day of the year. The Relay centre employs Slovenian Sign Language Interpreters and is FREE OF CHARGE for the users. It is financed by the Ministry of Labour, Family, Social Affairs and Equal Opportunities.

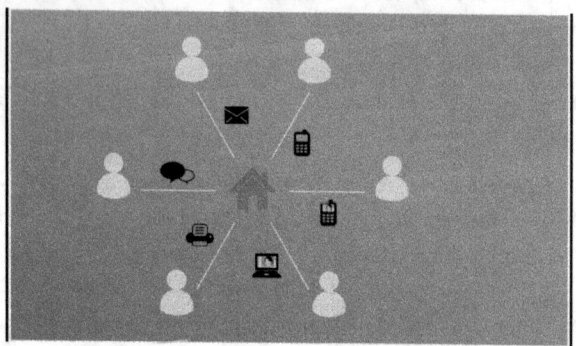

What does the relay centre provide?

The Relay centre for persons with hearing impairment requires registration and verification of the user solely on the grounds of his or her mobile number, making it very user-friendly. Its technical specification enables tracking (of content as well as the sequence of events) of all the relayed communications regardless of the communication channel, supervision of work process, the efficiency of the interpreters at the relay centre and the possibility of a statistical analysis based on a variety of criteria.

How to use the relay centre for persons with hearing impairment

Using the relay centre is very simple and user-friendly. The deaf and hearing-impaired person must register before first use. The users can register at the online address of the relay centre kc.tolmaci.si or with our Association or at their local association. The applicants need to fill in an application form with their name and family name, they can choose their own user name and password and write down their mobile phone number. After successful first registration, the deaf or hearing impaired first-time user receives an SMS with their unique user name and password and can start using the Relay centre immediately. All further communication is carried out directly via mobile phone, which provides greater flexibility for the user, or via the Relay centre website.

Benefits of the relay centre for persons with hearing impairment

We carried out a survey among the users of the relay centre about their satisfaction with the Relay centre service. The results showed that the users are very happy with the service, because a Slovenian Sign Language interpreter is available day or night, every day of the year. The users find that accessing certain types of information is much easier, because they can sort out their affairs 'from the couch', which saves travel and other problems. The choice of the communication channel is entirely up to them; they feel safe and independent and, last but not least, their privacy is guaranteed. The users believe that the bundle of all these benefits is a significant contribution to the improvement of their quality of life.

Skills the of Slovenian Sign Language Interpreters must master to work at the relay centre

Slovenian Sign Language Interpreters are trained to interpret from the spoken language into sign language and vice-versa. Work at the relay centre requires the interpreter to master specific knowledge and skills. The interpreters need good communication skills; they need to have a good sense of prediction, and of knowledge of where to direct the inquiries, because the user doesn't necessarily have all the relevant information at the first contact. Interpreters must also be resourceful, depending on the user and the addressee of the relay. The interpreters must also be responsive, because they need to follow the protocol and receive a »call« in the shortest possible time in the running order of the »calls« received. The interpreters do not have the possibility to prepare for the topic in advance because the »video calls« take place in real time. They are also required to be familiar with various types of public institutions, because certain users do not know which institution is able to answer their inquiry and expect the interpreter to know this. A mastery of written communication is also required, as well as the ability to understand text messages sent by the relay centre users. Certain users are not highly literate so their messages are incomprehensible to some, while the interpreter is required to understand the received text message and acquire the information the user requires. In order to give you a vague idea, here are some of the text messages of deaf users, which may be difficult to understand for those unfamiliar with the deaf population:

1. I am pain leg. When at time?
2. +3861xxxxxxxxx. Mine relay. Enough mine relay
3. Ask. Can old with new credit
4. Question can be cold ice tooth
5. Just now gotten home and reviewed bank statement because they need of social welfare.
6. Urgently tell lady boss. Today dog got operated. I need to examination. Tomorrow has check-up. Do I have go to work.
7. I am interested at what time working hours in centre possibilities
8. Good morning. Please you relay forestry inspection. Tell. You see our house near trees. Chimney sweeper very close. I not responsible. Please come see how come. That owner has nothing taken care of

The core activity of the relay centre is focused on the needs of the users. It is not uncommon for users to send questions in writing or forward a message, or a job application, letter, etc. with the request for us to make a the necessary corrections, which means that the interpreters need to be very fluent in Slovenian written language. We have also come across opposite, when deaf users turn to the Relay centre to help them translate the letters they have received from various institutions into Slovenian Sign Language.

In line with the results of the survey we carried out among the users of the Relay centre and the interpreters who work at the centre, we have found that the progress in information technology has contributed greatly to the the quality of life of the deaf community and removed many of the obstacles they previously faced on a daily basis. According to users, 'remote interpreting' is useful and very welcome if they need access to short pieces of information and relatively undemanding discussions. In other cases, prefer 'tête à tête' interpreting, as the presence of the interpreter itself gives them the feeling of safety on the one hand and, on the other, they can meet with the interpreter beforehand and discuss the topic of meeting or conversation. The interpreters who work at the relay centre are of the same opinion as the users, namely, they believe in the importance of being able to meet the user before the interpretation and of being in the same room so that they can see the whole interaction.

Hilde Haualand (Norway): Interpreting ideals and relaying rights

Hilde Haualand, researcher and social anthropologist at the Fafo Institute of Welfare and Social Research in Oslo, Norway. In her PhD dissertation (2012) she compared the video interpreting services in the USA, Sweden and Norway. Inspired by actor-network theory and the sociology of technology and science, she discussed the interplay between political decisions, technological solutions and the roles of interpreters and users of the video interpreting services in these countries. Previous research also includes disabled inmates in Norwegian prisons, disabled people and the labour market, GLBT-persons with a disability, the transnationalism of Deaf communities and more.

Contact details for correspondence: hilde.haualand@fafo.no

Abstract: The video interpreting service, which is primarily targeted at people who use sign language, and appears 'live' the moment it is performed, serves very different political goals in the USA, Sweden and Norway. In this presentation, the interplay between disability rights, political ideals and technical and organisational solutions (based on multi-sited fieldwork in the three countries) will be used to show that a service that appears the same across different countries, may distribute widely different rights, opportunities and roles to the actors involved, including the interpreters and the Deaf users/consumers/clients of the services. In the US, there is a clear financial, organisational and conceptual demarcation between what is termed Video Relay Service (VRS) and Video Remote Interpreting (VRI); a demarcation barely visible in Sweden and Norway. VRS is approaching a billion dollar market in the US and is considered a telecommunication service. In Norway, the entire service is organised and defined as an extension to the national interpreting service, while the Swedish system is characterised by a more ebalanced interaction between the telecommunication sector and sign language interpreting institutions. As a consequence, the Video Interpreting systems distribute different rights and represent different political ideals, and the roles performed by both the interpreters and the deaf people in these three countries are quite disimilar. The analysis is based on multi-sited fieldwork in the three countries from 2006-2010, and the research material includes interviews with a wide range of actors involved in providing, using and regulating the services, public documents (on paper and online) and notes from participant observations.

Video Interpreting Services

Video interpreting always involves a sign language interpreter who interprets conversations between a Deaf person using sign language and a hearing non-signer by way of a videophone, a studio and eventually a regular telephone if the parties communicating are at different locations. This similarity in the use or provision across different countries is paralleled by a striking diversity in terminology, financial mechanisms, regulations and dispersion of the service. A growing number of countries provide video interpreting services, but the definitions, scopes and organisation of the services vary greatly. These are the different definitions of video interpreting in the USA, Sweden and Norway, the services are defined in three different ways;

- "Video Relay Service (VRS) is a form of Telecommunications Relay Service (TRS) that enables persons with hearing disabilities who use American Sign Language (ASL) to communicate with voice telephone users through video equipment..." (Federal Communications Commission)(FCC, 2013)
- Bildtelefoni.net interprets conversations between people who use sign language and hearing people. The service provides relaying and remote interpreting by way of a videophone. (PTS, 2013)
- ...shall increase the users' access to interpreters and give greater opportunities for equality and participation in work life. The service is a supplement to other kinds of interpreting. (National Insurance Agency (NAV, 2013)

These definitions testify to the different goals the services have, despite the similarity of how the service is provided. In this presentation, I will show how a technology that is apparently the same, serves widely different goals in different social and political contexts. The video interpreting services may appear the same across different countries, but they distribute different rights, opportunities and roles to the participants involved, including the interpreters and the Deaf users/consumers/clients of the services.

These differences are one reason I use "video interpreting services" as the common name for these services, not "video relay services" (VRS), which is often used in 'international jargon'. In the US, VRS is limited to the provision of telecommunication services. Remote interpreting by way of videophones is not included in this definition, and is called Video Remote Interpreting. Some countries separate these two modes of video interpreting, while some do not. Hence, I have chosen the more "neutral" term video interpreting, if I am not talking specifically about VRS as it is understood by the Americans.

Method

As part of my doctorate research project in social anthropology, I studied the interaction between communication technologies, disability and politics in the US, Sweden and Norway (Haualand, 2010, 2011, 2012, forthcoming). The analysis is built on material gathered through a broad array of methods during fieldwork in these countries from 2005-2010.[i] I have observed, interviewed or talked with people about their use(s) of videophones and video interpreting services. I also visited companies, carried out formal and informal interviews, and analysed both printed and online documents and information from the US, Sweden and Norway. Last, but not least, I participated in several workshops and meetings hosted by major organisations involved in video interpreting where various actors involved in providing, regulating, using and/or financing video interpreting services discussed common matters of concern. These workshops were tangible manifestations of the video interpreting service networks in the three countries. The discussions with other participants were an invaluable source of information about the varying views of the relevant actors, stakeholders and target groups in each country. The fact that people were frequently puzzled by my questions and assertions was especially enlightening, since these responses revealed how and when both they and I took definitions, scopes and political goals for granted.

The American disability politics have traditionally put emphasis on implementing and enforcing civil rights and non-discriminating social regulations with the Americans with Disabilities Act (ADA) as the legal spearhead. In Norway and Sweden, individually anchored rights to social services and economical security are to a much larger extent implemented. The three current ways of implementing and organising the video interpreting services in those three countries, can easily be identified with, and perceived as a consequence of these legal conditions. The definition and organisation of the video interpreting services are on one hand shaped by the existing legal frameworks in the countries it is implemented. But on the other hand, these frameworks did not initiate the services, and the implementation of video interpreting is also a story about how technology shapes, reformulates and consolidates an existing political system.

USA

In the US, bulk of the discussion is related to the video relay services, which is defined as a telecommunication service to secure what is defined as a civil right; the right to functionally equivalent telecommunication services for all. All citizens have the right to use whatever telecommunication equipment they have (including videophones) to access various telecommunication services. The regulations for VRS are regularly amplified by the Federal Communications Commission (FCC) to secure the right to functionally equivalent telecommunication services for deaf and hearing impaired people, and the interpreters are there to secure this right. The provision of video interpreting services is organised as an open market, where the service providers must follow FCC regulations for reimbursement. The service providers compete to provide the most user friendly videophones and best qualified interpreters to capture as many customers as possible, in order to receive income from the telecommunication relay service fund financed by the telecommunication carriers.

With very few exceptions, VRS providers distribute videophones to the end users. Videophones are lent or given to the consumers, who only have to pay for their own connection to the telecommunication network. Lending videophones that are configured to easily connect to a particular service and complicates communication with other providers' services optimizes the payback of the investment in terminals, since it creates a loyalty, albeit sometimes mainly technical, to the provider who lends the equipment. The VRS providers are reimbursed from the Telecommunication Relay Service fund[1], and the amount is generated from the time

---

[1] The fund is financed through a fee that is added to every telecommunication client's telephone bill, not only those who use the relay services. In 2009, the contribution factor was

(minutes) the consumers use their services. Hence, the more clients that use the services of a particular VRS provider, the larger the amount reimbursed. The competition is directed towards Deaf consumers, and the companies compete in providing the most useful and user-friendly technology/videophones, as well as in providing the most qualified interpreters. Most providers have websites directed to their consumers, with slick welcome and advertising messages in American Sign Language (mostly by Deaf people) and English (and Spanish) text. The focus is on communication, convenient technical solutions and efficiency. The regulations have been amended to fit new technological opportunities, and the technology has undergone improvements and changes that are both a response to the demands from FCC (Interoperability between different phone models and service providers, monitoring, and regular, ten digit telephone numbers to name a few) and the consumers (user friendly interface, portability and more). Attempts to use the VRS for situations where Video Remote Interpreting or a community interpreter would have been more appropriate, is not tolerated. Being a telecommunication service, the sign language interpreters are called 'operators' or 'communication assistants', and the expenses are reimbursed in 'minutes'. The definition of VRS initially did not even mention the interpreter. The VRS providers compete with additional services like 'sign mail' (voice mail), video answering functions and inbuilt telephone lists.

While VRS is growing into a billion dollar industry in the USA, Video Remote Interpreting is only provided by a few companies, and is regulated and paid for the same as in other situations where the interpreter is physically present (community interpreting). Compared to the attention paid to Video Remote Interpreting, VRS related issues totally dominate the American video interpreting discourse.

Sweden

In Sweden, the political emphasis is on securing increased accessibility for deaf and hearing impaired people through telecommunication technologies. It is the possibilities the (new) technology provide, that is in the focus of the efforts. The video interpreting service is considered a governmental responsibility, and the public authority responsible for the telecommunication sector is also responsible for procuring and regulating the service. The service is operated by a public regional

---

0,01137% for every telephone bill. (Federal Communications Commission, 2009)

sign language interpreter agency that serves the whole country. Regional medical-rehabilitative authorities provide the videophones on basis of a medical certificate stating that a person has a severe hearing impairment. Deaf people receive a videophone at no cost, but only after an application has been signed by a physician or employer and approved by the regional authority.

The system is distinguished by a separation of the systems for provision of videophones and the service providers, which is possibly related to the relatively strong position of the videophone and communication technology developers in the country. Due to the procurement practice, potential video interpreting service providers do in principle compete against one another towards the procuring authority. There has however only been one provider of video interpreting services since 1997. Bildtelefoni.net has set up website (www.bildtelefoni.net) that is clearly directed at people using sign language as their primary language. The website is mainly informational; not aimed at recruiting more clients. There is no information about any equipment, except a FAQ-answer stating that the equipment provider provides technical support. The service is open to any user with compatible equipment (often developed in Sweden), and the distinction between VRS and VRI is not very prominent, except in statistical reports, which shows that around 75-80% of the assignments can be defined as video relay calls (Tolkcentralen, 2010). The demand is growing steadily, and at peak hours, there may be hour-long queues. In USA, the VRS providers are subject to strict response- and delay rules, which are pursuant to VRS' main function – functionally equivalent telecommunication services. In Sweden, the issue is accessibility to telecommunication services – which does not automatically entail functional equivalence[2]. But since Swedish video interpreting not is confined to secure functionally equivalent telecommunication services, there is room for more divergent – yet still intersecting interests from the various actors involved. To the regional authorities and public interpreter providers, video interpreting is a tool to make their services available in sign language more accessible and efficient, to the telecom authority, the VRS secures access to telecommunication services (which is their responsibility, cf. The sector responsibility principle), the engineers are securing a market for their products (the videophones) and Deaf people experience that they can use the telecommunication

---

[2] There are rules for maximum response time in the procurement documents, but the time from the caller is connected to the service to a sign language interpreter actually is available, is in practice much longer, especially at peak hours.

network for communication in a verbal[3] language, as well as requeting interpreter services on an ad hoc basis.

Norway

I will now turn to Norway – where the government and political system like Sweden is of the social democratic type (cf. Esping-Andersen, 1990), but where the video interpreting is not associated with a telecommunication issue at all. The Norwegian video interpreting service is organised as an extension of the national sign language interpreter service under the National Insurance Agency, and the telecommunication sector is not involved. Anyone entitled to sign language interpreter services as stipulated in the National Insurance Act may use the service. Dedicated videophones are only distributed to work places where there is a deaf person entitled to interpreter services, and to persons under 26 years old. All other deaf people (entitled to receive interpreter services) may apply for a licence to download software to their computer.

References to telecommunication or accessibility in general are infinitesimal, even though 75% of the assignments are relayed telephone calls (NAV, 2010). The service is the youngest of the three compared here, and is steadily increasing the operation hours, and will run from 8-20 by mid-September 2013. There are no rules on answering times. The National Insurance Agency distributes several of the same videophones as are marketed in Sweden, but in the application forms, this is called equipment for video interpreting[4]. What is defined as a communication technology device in Sweden and USA is defined as an instrument to access the interpreter service in Norway. The National Insurance Agency also gives information about the service on their website, but it takes several clicks (and knowledge about the existence of the service) to get there. The short bullet point text on their website seems to be directed at employers, but there is a video that can be played in a new window explaining in sign language how the service works. In the movie, the interpreter walks to the studio when a Deaf person calls to request an interpreter, a delay that is considered a violation of the VRS regulations in USA, but indeed confirms the Norwegian view that video interpreting is an extension or a supplement to the regular interpreter service.

---

[3] "Verbal" as in opposition to "written" language, not referring to the modality visual vs auditive
[4] Utstyr for bildetolking

Relayed Rights

As a consequence, the Video Interpreting systems distribute different rights and represent different political ideals, and the roles performed by both the interpreters and the deaf people in these three countries are not the same. In the US, the video relay service is defined as a means to achieve functionally equivalent telecommunication services for all. The service providers have to compete for each client, and Deaf people are treated like consumers, who are free to choose one or more VRS providers. Both the quality of the interpreters and innovative technological solutions are used to market the services, but it is the deaf consumers who are the target of the service. The interpreters are not a means per se, but a tool to secure functional equivalence for all. In this system, there is no room for using interpreters for anything else other than securing functionally equivalent telecommunication services, so remote interpreting and any other use of interpreters via videophones are delegated to other community sectors and service providers. There are also signs that the VRS-industry employs so many interpreters that the overall access to interpreters in schools, hospitals and other situations where community interpreting is requested, has declined. Also, the working conditions and code of conduct of the interpreters is under pressure from demands from the service providers (Peterson, 2011). While the deaf consumer may experience better access to telecommunication services, the interpreters are probably facing tougher working conditions (Dean, Pollard, & Samar, 2010; Peterson, 2011).

As a contrast to the consumer-centered service in the US, is the Norwegian service with its explicit focus on providing interpreter services. The technology (videophones) is defined as a tool to access the interpreter service, and is not administered as a telecommunication device. Also, it is an extension to the traditional interpreter service (community interpreting), and the telecommunication sector has not been involved in developing the service. Deaf people in Norway do probably have some of the most extensive rights to interpreter services in the world (despite quite a few shortcomings, like lack of sufficient interpreters to meet the demand and lack of shift work schemes that severely restricts the availability of interpreters after office hours), and the video interpreter service is organised to secure this right. There is no organisational or practical separation between VRS and remote interpreting. The political motivation to initiate the service was first to improve access to interpreters in the work place. Still, only deaf people at work may receive dedicated desktop videophones, but everyone with compatible software may use the video interpreting service. The interpreters work both as community interpreters and video interpreters, and there are no separate payment schemes. The situation for the interpreters is probably more satisfying in Norway than in the US. The end users do however experience limited access in several ways. It is not always possible to use the videophones to call directly to another videophone. Also, the service was first targeted at deaf people who already had a job, not those outside the labour market. A few years later, deaf people could apply for and receive a license to download software to their private computers. Since the access to user friendly and simple videophones is restricted to people at work, and it requires some computer knowledge, the service is mostly accessible to literate deaf people, but not to those who might need sign language interpreting the most – those with limited knowledge in written Norwegian and older people with limited computer experience. The service is however growing steadily, but it is still organised as a tool to get in touch with interpreters. A major question that could be asked in regard to the Norwegian system is whether the video interpreter service is a tool to access interpreters – or if it is a tool to secure accessibility and equality for Deaf people. If it is the latter, there should be much more focus on recruiting more clients, and to make the service more efficient in terms of the time it takes to set up a call, and technical accessibility.

If it is possible to establish a continuum, the Swedish system may be placed somewhere between the American and Norwegian systems for video interpreting. The Swedes have organised the service as a means to increase accessibility for Deaf and hard of hearing people, by way of telecommunication technology and interpreters. Hence, the interpreters and end users may have a more equal status, since the service is not specifically targeted at either group. There is also a long tradition for trials and development of communication technologies in Sweden, so there have been trials to extend the video interpreting service to public offices, where it can be activated when a Deaf person comes to the counter (after some time in a queue), and tri-party emergency calls (Brugnoli, Delprato, Marconi, & Hellström, 2012). With a broader definition than in the US and Norway, the deaf end users may inhabit more roles than merely being a telecommunication consumer or a user of interpreter services. The focus on technology development puts Deaf people in the role of experts. The videophones are however, in terms of dispersion, considered as medical-rehabilitation technology, and in order to receive a videophone, a physician must sign the application that documents a "medical need" for a videophone. The service itself is set up to improve accessibility and enhance communication between deaf and hearing people, but it does not have any specific references to standards like "functional equivalence". In Norway, the service is tied to each deaf individual's right to receive interpreter services, but this is not the case in Sweden. It is hence a general accessibility service, which indeed seems to work well and is very popular, but does also mean heavy queues at peak hours and, as it is not running 24/7, the accessibility it offers is still limited.

In Norway, it is defined as an extension of the sign language interpreter service. The three countries are fairly similar with regard to the social status of disabled people, living conditions and telecommunication infrastructure. But almost twenty years after the first video interpreting trials in these three countries, video interpreting approaches a billion dollar market in the USA, is subject to heavy demand (including long queues) in Sweden, while the service is still in its infancy with limited outreach and requests in Norway, at least compared to the two other countries.

Politics is performed through a variety of services and institutions, and few, if any of these have been established in a political vacuum. If it is indeed a goal to develop and establish video interpreting services, one should also discuss what goal the service should have, and what the primary task is. Is it to improve overall accessibility, increase access to interpreters or to make telecommunication services available to deaf people? Does the system, and the way the services are organised, promote all of these, or only some?

List of references

Brugnoli, M. C., Delprato, U., Marconi, P., & Hellström, G. (2012). REACH112 responding to All Citizens Needing Help - Final Project Report. In Reach 112 (Ed.).

Dean, R., Pollard, R., & Samar, V. (2010). RID research grant underscores occupational health risks: VRS and K-12 settings most concerning. VIEWS, 27(1), 41-43.

Esping-Andersen, G. (1990). The three worlds of welfare capitalism. Cambridge: Polity Press.

FCC. (2013). Video Relay Services, 2013, from http://www.fcc.gov/guides/video-relay-services

Haualand, H. (2010). Provision of Videophones and Video Interpreting for the Deaf and Hard of Hearing Stockholm: Hjälpmedelinstitutet.

Haualand, H. (2011). Interpreted Ideals and Relayed Rights - Video Interpreting Services as Objects of Politics. Disability Studies Quarterly, 31(4).

Haualand, H. (2012). Interpreting Ideals and Relaying Rights - A comparative Study of Video Interpreting Services in Norway, Sweden and the United States. Philosophiae Doctor, University of Oslo Oslo (346)

Haualand, H. (forthcoming). Video Interpreting Services: Calls for Inclusion or Redialling Exclusion? Ethnos.

NAV. (2010). Sum anrop. In J. Hansen (Ed.), (E-mail ed.). Oslo NAV.

NAV. (2013). Bildetolktjenesten, 2013, from
http://www.nav.no/helse/hjelpemidler/tolketjenesten/183114.cms

Peterson, R. (2011). Profession in pentimento; A narrative inquiry into interpreting in video settings. In B. Nicodemus & L. Swabey (Eds.), Advances in Interpreting Research - Inquiry in action Amsterdam: John Benjamins.

PTS. (2013). Bildtelefoni.net, 2013, from
http://www.pts.se/sv/Privat/Telefoni/Tjanster-for-aldre-och-personer-med-funktionsnedsattning-/Bildtelefoninet/

Tolkcentralen. (2010). Statistik förmedlingstjänsten per studio infomega.se. Örebro.

Peter Llewellyn-Jones (UK): The impact of monological interpreting models approaches when applied to remote interpretations

Peter Llewellyn-Jones, is a founder member of the UK's Register of Sign Language Interpreters and ASLI. Peter is a Visiting Research Fellow at the University of Leeds Centre for Translation Studies. He also teaches Interpreting Theory to spoken language conference, community and diplomatic interpreters in the UK, Europe and China. Having published papers and book chapters on all aspects of interpreting, his new book, Redefining the Role of the Community Interpreter (co-written with Robert G. Lee) is due to be published by SLI Press later this year.

Contact details for correspondence: p.llewellyn-jones@slilimited.co.uk

Abstract: Recent research carried out by the University of Surrey into videoconference spoken language interpretations (Braun and Taylor 2012) found that there were significantly more interpreting errors and misunderstandings during remotely interpreted police interviews than when control interviews were carried out face-to-face. Many of the problems were those that arise in any dialogical interpretation but there were more of them when the interpreter wasn't present. This paper will explore whether one reason for this is that videoconference/remote interpreting technology, and the expectations of its users, restrict interpreters to using a monological interpreting approach rather than the more dialogical, interactive approach that is typical of face-to-face communicative events.

By examining data from both spoken language and signed language remote interpretations and from signed-spoken language telephone interpretations, the paper will go on to look at how possible it might be to mitigate these problems by changing the expectations of the commissioners and re-thinking the communicative behaviours of the interpreters.

Reference: Braun, S. And Taylor, J. (2012) www.videoconference-interpreting.net

Remote Interpreting and its Impact on Dialogical Interactions

Whilst telephone interpreting for Deaf interlocutors has long been an accepted and commonplace occurrence, more recent advances in technology have allowed for the development and increasing use of other forms of long-distance electronic communication. That Deaf communities (in the more developed countries, at least) have embraced the development of web-based video communication is not surprising. They can, at long last, engage in direct screen-to-screen (if not face-to-face) communication with fellow signed language users as easily as non-Deaf people can use the telephone. Neither is it surprising that the same technology has been adopted as a medium for providing interpreting services. The arguments for providing web-based 'remote' or 'videoconference' interpreting services are compelling: availability of interpreters where none are available locally, cost, speed, etc. A new industry has emerged with local organisations and private companies, both national and international, offering instant access to interpreters so that minority language users can access public services and, in the case of Deaf people, book appointments with service providers, contact non-Deaf relatives, friends and colleagues, etc.

It is inevitable that as new services are established in different countries, a variety of terms will spring up to describe them; for example Video Relay Service (VRS) is the preferred term for web-based sign language interpreting services in the USA as well as with some service providers in the UK (Association of Sign Language Interpreters' VRS policy statement, 2013) and Sweden (Warnick and Plejert, 2012), and the terms Videoconference and Remote Interpreting have been used in Europe and elsewhere to differentiate between situations where the interpreter is with one of the interlocutors, with the other participant(s) linked by video technology from a separate location (videoconference) and when the interlocutors are either in the presence of each other (e.g. A doctor and patient, or a lawyer and client) or themselves in separate locations and relying on a video feed of an interpreter from another location altogether (remote).

Of interest here, though, is what happens to the role-spaces (Llewellyn-Jones and Lee, in press) available to the interpreter during non-face-to-face interpreted interactions. Role-space, briefly, is the room for manoeuvre the interpreter has, in terms of behaviour, in the various interactions within which they work. The space comprises the three-dimensional shape delineated by points along three axes:

X. The axis of participant/conversational alignment (sociolinguistic and psycholinguistic)
Y. The axis of interaction management
Z. The axis of 'presentation of self'

(Llewellyn-Jones and Lee, in press)[5]

Llewellyn-Jones and Lee have shown that, for an interpreted telephone call to be anything other than extremely awkward for at least one of the interlocutors, the interpreter has to manage the call, both overtly and covertly, and make a particular effort to jointly construct meaning with the interlocutor who isn't physically present, and this requires a degree of 'presentation of self' (Goffman, 1990) on the part of the interpreter. There are some interpreting settings, though, where the interpreter is expected to be 'in the background' and not overtly influence the communicative interaction.

The European Commission's AVIDICUS project funded a consortium of universities to conduct research into the effectiveness and reliability or otherwise of using videoconference and remote interpreting in the justice system. Surrey University, with the cooperation of London's Metropolitan Police Force, looked specifically at the use of web-based technology for the provision of interpretation in police stations (English – French); Lessius University College in Antwerp conducted research into the use of similar technology in police interviews in Belgium and in the Netherlands (Dutch – Hungarian); and a third consortium member, TEPIS (the Polish Society of Sworn and Specialised Translators), conducted research into Prosecutors' examinations of witnesses in Poland (Polish - English). The first report

---

[5] This text has been published since the 2013 efsli conference (see bibliography).

of the project's findings (Braun, et al., 2011) also included a paper by Jemina Napier (then of Macquarie University) that reported on a study into the effectiveness of videoconference and remote sign language interpreter provision in courts in New South Wales. All of these studies reported that, provided that the picture and sound quality were good, it was possible for interpreters to understand the interlocutors and produce complete renditions of the spoken/signed utterances that were, in turn, understood by the respective interlocutors.

All of the studies did, though, also identify problems. Analysis of the police station interviews recorded by the Surrey University team showed that, although the problems encountered by the interpreter when working under videoconference or remote conditions were similar to those that normally arise in face-to-face interpretations (for example, the need to ask that an utterance is repeated or clarified) there were significantly more of these instances when communicating via the web-based technology.

To summarise the findings, compared to (the control) face-to-face interactions, the videoconference/remote modes of working resulted in:

- Inaccuracies 124%
- Omissions 124%
- Additions 290%
- Linguistic problems: lexis/terminology, Idiomaticity, grammar, style/register, Coherence, language mixing 127%
- Paralinguistic problems 1: articulation, Hesitation, repetition 132%
- Paralinguistic problems 2: false start, self-repair 110%
- Synchronisation problems (turn-taking) 324%

(after Braun and Taylor, 2011)

The biggest difference in incidence rate was that of the synchronisation of turns. The other studies also reported problems with synchronisation and the consensus reached by the AVIDICUS research teams was that the problem stemmed from either the interpreter or one of the interlocutors not being able to see all the other interlocutors. In the New South Wales experiments, the interpreters and Deaf interlocutors were asked to comment on their experiences. Some of their responses merit quoting at length.

- (Scenario 1: Deaf defendant) [They] could have three coloured lights to help indicate who is speaking. For example, if the Judge is speaking, then one light lights up to indicate this. I'm only suggesting this because when looking at the small screen it can be quite difficult to know who is speaking, which can be confusing.
  - (Scenario 1: Interpreter) I think it's important to have the hearing people on screen, just to get in your own head where they are, who they are, rather than just hearing voices. Because sometimes you can't discriminate the voices.
  - (Scenario 2: Interpreter) I don't need to see me, but it was helpful being able to see the Judge. It would have been helpful to see the Prosecutor. … I was not sure if she was asking a question of [the Deaf defendant] and then it made me think I'd interpreted incorrectly. But then she started talking and I was like, "Oh! There's someone else here."
  - (Scenario 2: Deaf defendant) Having the large TV screen on the far wall, opposite the Witness Box was good, but it wasn't always clear who was speaking – if it was the Judge or one of the solicitors. Working through the AVL, I don't think the interpreter was fully aware of the positioning of people within the courtroom so wasn't able to convey it clearly. For it to work effectively, you'd have to clearly inform the interpreter about who is in the courtroom and where they were positioned. Because the interpreter is conveying the speech from all the other participants, and without clearly establishing who is speaking, it is remarkably confusing.

(Napier 2011: 169)

The problem of not being able to see all the participants was also highlighted in an interpreted exchange recorded by the Lessius team.

In the experiment involving a VCI B setting – a case of the criminal conspiracy – the interpreter was together with the suspect while the police officer was alone in a remote location. The interpreter was sitting behind the suspect so that the suspect could not see the interpreter. The suspect was clearly disturbed by this set up and always turned towards the interpreter when speaking.

(Balogh and Hertog, 2011)

After a fairly protracted interpreted exchange between the police offer and the suspect, it was agreed that she could move her chair so that she could see the interpreter.

Although she still did not gaze at the interpreter, it seemed to be necessary for her to see the person who was speaking.

(ibid.)

It would appear that the constraints of the technology lead to a lack of access to, or a much reduced awareness of, the non-verbal cues of the interlocutors and, as Llewellyn-Jones and Lee (in press) have noted, it is the simultaneous feedback, both verbal and non-verbal, that allows the co-construction of meaning (see, for example, Garrod and Pickering 2007). In other words, it is as if the technology and the participants' reaction to it result in the exchange of short-chunk monological utterances and responses rather than dialogical interactions. If this is the case, this might explain the increase in 'problem/error' rate because the interlocutors aren't, at least not effortlessly, creating a shared 'situation', or co-constructing meaning.

Comparison of interpreting modes in collaborative interactions

To test this hypothesis, it was arranged to observe and record a variety of interpreted interactions at Signing Network, a cooperative established by a group of qualified interpreters in the city of Leicester (UK). Rather than the more formal or, even, formulaic discourse varieties that typify legal settings, interpreters were observed dealing with a range of less formal enquiries and spontaneous interactions over the course of three of their weekly 'open house' or drop-in days when local

Deaf people can come into the offices to have letters translated or telephone calls interpreted free of charge.

Rather than as an empirical, quantitative study, the research was designed as an ethnographic observation/qualitative study to determine how telephone/video remote interpreting differs from face-to-face interpreting in terms of:

1. Interlocutor – interpreter alignment
2. Interlocutor – interlocutor alignment
3. The impact of one or more of the participants not being able to see the visual back-channelling cues of all of the other participants and how this effects the interaction skills/communicative competence of the participants

Those who willingly participated in this small-scale study included Deaf colleagues from the Leicester Deaf Action Group (LDAG) which shares the office premises with the interpreters' cooperative, Deaf service users who had received forms or letters that required a written or telephone response and a range of non-signing 'hearing' people, both professionals (e.g. Social workers) and students, who came to enquire about the services offered. The Deaf Directors of LDAG also volunteered to take part in spontaneous discussions and conversations to afford the opportunity to record sufficient samples of different modes of interpreting.

The interpreters and participants/interlocutors were asked to take part in three types of interaction:

1. Face-to-face interactions between Deaf and non-Deaf interlocutors
2. Interpreted telephone calls for Deaf individuals needing to contact external organisations and companies
3. Conversations between Deaf and hearing interlocutors facilitated by a remote interpreter linked by a computer and webcam

All of the Deaf people who participated were either Directors, members of staff or frequent visitors to the office who knew the interpreters well and worked with them on a regular basis. It was also made it clear that, during the interactions, either the interlocutors or interpreters could ask for the recording to stop or if, after the event, they realised that any sensitive or confidential matters had arisen, that the recordings be erased.

Over two and a half days a total of eight completed interactions and one abandoned interaction were video-recorded (excluding false starts and remotely interpreted interactions that had to be halted because of deterioration in picture quality when the internet feed was interrupted or there was a drop in download speed).

1. Face-to-face discussion between a male Deaf Director of LDAG and a male student from a local college who came to ask about problems Deaf people face accessing the accident and emergency department of the local hospital.
    I. Duration 2' 38"
    II. Interpreter A

2. Face-to-face discussion between a female Deaf Director and a female social worker who had called in to ask about the services available during the weekly 'open house' drop-in sessions
    I. Duration 7' 30"
    II. Interpreter B

3. Face-to-face discussion between a female 'hearing', non-signing administrator and a Deaf woman who had called in to ask the service to contact a local Roman Catholic church to enquire about the possibility of her daughter attending Communion preparation classes
    I. Duration 5' 46"
    II. Interpreter C

4. Telephone-interpreted call to the priest of a local Roman Catholic church to enquire about Communion preparation classes
    I. Duration 5' 56"
    II. Interpreter C

5. Telephone-interpreted call from a female LDAG Director to a city police station to speak to the Community Police Officer responsible for arranging a Deaf Awareness Course being provided by LDAG

I. Duration 3' 32"
   II. Interpreter B

6. Telephone-interpreted call to an insurance company to enquire about a pension plan applied for by a male Deaf service user
   I. Duration 4' 45"
   II. Interpreter A

7. Remote-interpreted discussion between the male Deaf leader of the LDAG 'job-club' and a female hearing interlocutor who had called into the office to make enquiries about the services it offers
   I. Duration 11' 36"
   II. Interpreter A

8. Remote-interpreted discussion between a male Deaf Director and a female non-signing administrator about a letter he had received regarding his up-coming state pension entitlement
   I. Duration 11' 20"
   II. Interpreter A

9. Remote-interpreted conversation between a middle-aged female Deaf person who had called in for coffee and a female 'hearing' non-signing volunteer who was asking questions about LDAG's weekly, social coffee mornings which are held in a room above the offices
   I. Duration 5' 49"
   II. Interpreter D

The nine interactions were interpreted by three experienced, qualified interpreters and Directors of Signing Network (A, B, C) and a less experienced qualified interpreter who works occasionally for the cooperative (D).

   A. Male; approximately fifteen years of interpreting experience
   B. Female; approximately fifteen years of interpreting experience
   C. Female; approximately eight years of interpreting experience
   D. Female; approximately four years of interpreting experience

After each interaction, all of the participants (except the external interlocutors who were contacted by telephone) were asked to comment on the experience, how well it went, how satisfied they were with the outcome and process and to detail any problems they had noticed while taking part. These conversations were video-recorded.

Observations

The three interpreted telephone calls are described and discussed in some detail in Llewellyn-Jones and Lee (in press). For the purposes of this paper, though, the focus is on the differences between the face-to-face interactions (scenarios 1, 2 and 3) and those interpreted remotely via web-based video technology (scenarios 7, 8 and 9).

The first three (face-to-face) interactions produced little that the participants wanted to comment on. Seated informally around a table, the positioning of the interpreters - equidistant from the two principal interlocutors - allowed all three participants to see each other easily and it was noticeable that during the interactions all three naturally looked at whichever one of them was taking the floor whilst regularly glancing at the co-interlocutor or interpreter to monitor any back-channelling or simultaneous feedback. In none of the interactions did the interpreter have to manage turn-taking overtly.

In interaction 1, when the Deaf interlocutor talked about the problem of waiting to be seen in accident and emergency departments because of the difficulty of finding an interpreter to come out straight away, the hearing interlocutor interjected with "that's dreadful". The interpreter allowed the overlapping talk by momentarily pausing the sign-speech rendition, signing the interjection, then immediately resuming the original rendition whilst signalling to the Deaf interlocutor that he still had the floor so could continue with his turn. Neither the Deaf nor the hearing interlocutor noticed this covert management move. In the follow-up interview, the Deaf interlocutor, when asked to describe the interaction, signed "three of us conversation, good ... relaxed."

In terms of alignment, the interpreter was aligning equally with both of the principal interlocutors through visual cues (nods, smiles, etc.) And signed and spoken phatics as and when appropriate. This simultaneous feedback required a degree of presentation of self (e.g. Showing personal interest in the contributions of both interlocutors) and, at a sociolinguistic level, the interpreter's convergence (Giles, et al., 1991) with both interlocutors through slight shifts in body posture and the use of similar vocabulary items (signs and words). At the start of the interaction, the hearing interlocutor was clearly the least relaxed of the three, possibly because

1. He was not as used to interpreted interactions
2. He was considerably younger than both the Deaf interlocutor and the interpreter
3. He was the 'outsider' (the Deaf interlocutor and interpreter, sharing office space, were clearly friends and colleagues)

By the end of the relatively short interaction he was noticeably more relaxed and keen to find out more and this was undoubtedly, at least in part, due to the obviously friendly disposition of the interpreter. The convergent behaviours of the interpreter, coupled with the covert, conversational manner of his management of the conversational turns, no doubt contributed to the relaxed nature of the interaction. By the end of the conversation all three had adopted the same body positioning; leaning back slightly in their seats, smiling and nodding at each other.

Figure 1: Interaction 1 (interpreter left of screen; Deaf interlocutor seated centre-screen; hearing interlocutor with back to camera right of screen)

Interaction 2 was a face-to-face discussion interpreted by interpreter B. The opening turn was taken by the Deaf interlocutor and the interpreter started in third-person with "(name) said she met you ... how long ago was it now? ... She can't remember ..." to which the hearing interlocutor replied "about two or three weeks ago, was it? At the ULO [User-Led Organisations] event?" From then on the interpreter moved to using direct speech which, as the interlocutors were used to working with interpreters, seemed appropriate. All three adopted an equidistant seating plan around a table and it was noticeable that they were all aware of each other's visual feedback cues. The Deaf interlocutor looked mostly at the interpreter but regularly glanced and smiled at the hearing participant (usually after she had finished signing and was waiting for the interpreter to finish her spoken rendition). The hearing interlocutor, conversely, looked at the Deaf interlocutor most of the time, particularly when she was speaking herself, and tended to look at the interpreter only when the interpreter started talking or looked at her. Throughout the interaction there were several instances of overlapping-talk, all initiated by the hearing interlocutor anticipating how the interpreter was going to finish her spoken renditions. These were always managed by the interpreter continuing to hold the floor until she had finished (a maximum of two seconds) before beginning to interpret the hearing interlocutor's contributions. After the third or fourth occurrence it might have been easier if the interpreter had used a more overt management move, e.g. Asking the hearing participant to wait for a few seconds, and this was raised during the post-recording discussion.

Figure 2: Interaction 2 (Deaf interlocutor left of screen: interpreter centre-screen)

There were very few comments after the event other than "went well" from the Deaf interlocutor and "I found it very helpful" from the social worker. The interpreter said it was "fine, it's what we do nearly every day." When asked about the overlapping-talk, the interpreter explained that it was fairly easy to deal with so she didn't think it worth interrupting the flow to ask the social worker to wait.

In interaction 3, a face-to-face meeting between a hearing administrator and a Deaf person who had called in to ask for help to arrange Communion classes for her daughter, interpreter C also chose to sit at a table so that the participants were equidistant from each other and could easily see any visual communication and feedback cues. The interaction ran smoothly and was successful in that the Deaf person was able to explain what she wanted, resulting in it being agreed that the interpreter would facilitate a telephone call to the priest of the Deaf person's local Catholic Church. What was noticeable was that the interpreter glanced at the hearing interlocutor so often - even when she was simultaneously interpreting the Deaf interlocutor's contributions – that, on three occasions, she missed some of what was being signed and had to ask the signing interlocutor to repeat herself. This seems a fairly basic mistake for an experienced interpreter to make but it might well have been a result of the observer effect.

As the data collected was, in the main, naturally occurring and not under strict experimental conditions, it was impossible to predict the nature of the interactions and the order in which they would occur. Consequently, the interpreter had been party to some of the earlier post-recording discussions where the natural exchange of glances between the participants had been mentioned on several occasions as an important feature of face-to-face interactions. It is highly likely that this influenced the interpreter's behaviour during this interaction.

Interactions 7, 8 and 9 were all remotely interpreted, with the interpreters (A and C) sitting in a separate office linked to the interlocutors via a webcam. Two of the calls, 7 and 8, were made via 'Skype', and call 9 used 'oovoo'. The interpreters and interlocutors used different combinations of display screens; ipad to 15" laptop (interaction 7), ipad to ipad (interaction 8) and 15" laptop to 17" laptop (interaction 9).

Whether using the ipads or the larger screens of the laptops, all of the participants found that picture quality was not an issue and, providing the internet connection speed was fast enough, they were able to see and understand each other's sign language contributions quite easily.

Interaction 7 involved a question and answer session between a visitor and the Deaf employee who runs the weekly 'job club' organised by LDAG and the interpreters' cooperative. The hearing visitor started quite formally by saying "I wanted you to tell me about the job club. I know you are involved with the job club here." The Deaf interlocutor then started to explain how it worked and the types of activities and services available to unemployed Deaf people. The next question was "How many Deaf people come, would you say?" Other questions included "Is it the same Deaf people who come every week?", "Have you got any records of how many people have got jobs? Do you keep any records?" and "Are they temporary jobs or permanent jobs?" The Deaf interlocutor gave full answers to all of the questions and the visitor closed the interaction with "Thank you [name] and thank you [name] for interpreting." The Deaf person then thanked the visitor and the interpreter added "It was nice to meet you."

Figure 3: Interaction 7: (Deaf interlocutor back to camera; hearing interlocutor right of screen; the interpreter on screen)

(As can be seen from the screen shot above (Figure 3) the quality of the on-screen interpreter image was such that the Deaf interlocutor didn't even bother to resize the image to full-screen, saying that he could see it perfectly adequately.)

There were no turn taking problems and no examples of overlapping talk. The Deaf interlocutor, when signing his responses, regularly looked at the hearing visitor but, when she was speaking, fixed his gaze on the simultaneous interpretation on the screen. The spoken interpretation was, on occasions, a little hesitant; as if the interpreter was trying to find the best way of expressing what had been signed and the reason for this became clear during the post-recording interview.

When the interpreter joined the interlocutors in the main room he laughed and exclaimed "Oh, it was you!" As the hearing 'visitor' wasn't visible on the interpreter's screen, he explained that he had spent most of the time trying to guess who it might be. She had sounded well educated and, unable to see her body language or facial expressions, her questions seemed both informed and fairly formal. This led to the interpreter wondering whether this was a conversation motivated simply by her interest in the activities of LDAG or whether she was, in fact, doing an appraisal of the service for one of the funding bodies. Hence, he explained, his lack of confidence in how he was designing the spoken renditions. The Deaf interlocutor said that he felt a good rapport with the interpreter but didn't feel he was having a three way conversation, just responding to a series of questions, and the hearing participant said that she had felt completely left out when the Deaf person was looking at the screen. She couldn't see the interpreter because she would have had to sit too close to the Deaf person to see it easily and so her only contact with the interpreter was being able to hear him speak. She also noticed that the interpreter continued to speak, often for a few seconds, after the Deaf participant had finished signing and, during these periods, she looked at the Deaf participant but he didn't reciprocate, just continued to watch the screen. The video recordings showed that, during these extended spoken utterances, the interpreter signed the gist of what he was saying to show the Deaf person how far he had got with the interpretation and how he was finishing 'his' turn. This worked well for the Deaf interlocutor but not for the hearing interlocutor. She explained that she didn't feel that she was having a natural conversation and wouldn't have wanted it to continue any longer.

As a lead into interaction 8, the Deaf participant explained that he had received a letter from the UK Government's Department of Work and Pensions about claiming his pension entitlement when he reached retirement age the following year and wanted to ask the LDAG administrator whether he needed to do anything about it now. Interpreter A agreed to interpret the interaction remotely from his office and he and the Deaf interlocutor linked their ipads via the internet. What hadn't been anticipated at this stage was that this would be the most complicated of all of the interactions in terms of technology.

Figure 4: Interaction 8 (Deaf interlocutor left of screen; hearing (non-signing) administrator centre-screen; interpreter on screen)

The Deaf participant started by addressing the interpreter, "Hi, I just wanted to explain to her [indicates where she is sitting], [administrator's name], about ... er ... pensions [looking at the letter] it wants to know which bank ... they should sent it to ... I don't understand. Can you explain that to [name]?" He then hands the letter to the administrator who is sitting to his left, out of view of the interpreter. She then explains that the letter is saying that he is approaching the time when he can claim a pension or 'pension credit' and the letter is asking that he gives the Pension Service a call to "chat" about it. She pointed out that there was a 'text number' for people with 'hearing difficulties' and finished her turn with "and that's just about it." The Deaf interlocutor explained that he no longer had a 'mini-com' (text-phone) and asked whether she (the administrator) "could give them a call?" to which she responded "Oh, I could do. What, now?" As she dialled the number she commented that "this is all a bit new for me." After dialling the number, there was a wait of 2' 50" until the administrator was able to talk to an 'advisor'. During the wait, the administrator explained that she was going through the process of selecting from a range of options and that she wanted to speak to a person, rather than get a recorded message and, at one point, explained that she was now listening to some music. The Deaf participant initiated a conversation with the interpreter about the quality of the picture (which was good) and then asked the administrator, through the interpreter, whether she would need his bank card with his account details. She explained that this call was just about when he would be entitled to claim, to which he replied "Next year, I think."

On being connected to the 'advisor' the administrator explained the reason for the call and quoted sections of the letter, including a sentence that noted that they had tried to telephone him but were unable to get a reply. To this she explained that he is a "Deaf gentleman" and then asked "How old are you at the moment [name]? I'm sorry, I'm just speaking to him though a sign language interpreter." There then followed a (partly) interpreted telephone conversation lasting 4' 27" with the administrator relaying the spoken responses from the remote interpreter. She used third-person (reported speech) throughout the exchanges, "They are asking …." and "He's just saying that …", etc. She then explained that she was being put through to another department that might be able to help. She then listened to another advisor for approximately 50", occasionally saying "yes", "that's right" and turned to the Deaf interlocutor to say "Just bear with me a second, [name]." She then wrote some details on a piece of paper and after enquiring whether he could start the claim process now, ended the call by saying "That's great. I'll let him know. Thank you, bye-bye." She then hung up and turned to the Deaf participant to explain what had been said, i.e. That she had taken a note of a different telephone number that she needed to call to explain that he was Deaf and to ask that they send him a form (or she could ask them to email one) and that he was eligible to claim now so that his pension would be paid from the date of his next birthday. The Deaf participant then agreed that she should call the new number and she asked for his national insurance number as she would need it when she called. He pointed to the number on the top of the letter, then finger-spelled and signed it to the interpreter. The interpreter then spoke the number for the benefit of the administrator but had to ask twice for clarification of whether one of the finger-spelled letters was a 'B' or a 'D'. This interpretation wasn't necessary because the administrator had finished copying the number down from the original letter before the interpreted rendition was completed. At 11' 22" the researcher intervened to say that there was enough data and that the video recorder could be switched off.

In the ensuing discussion, the Deaf participant said that he thought it had all worked very well and he made a point of thanking the administrator for her help. The interpreter commented that, as he couldn't see the administrator, he could only go on what he could hear but the Deaf person seemed happy with the outcome so it seemed to be a successful interaction. Both the Deaf interlocutor and the interpreter agreed that it hadn't felt like a 'conversation' because they had to wait for the administrator to finish the call and explain what needed to happen next. It was noticeable that the Deaf interlocutor only looked at the administrator when he passed her the letter and, towards the end of the interaction, when he pointed to his

National Insurance number. For the rest of the time he concentrated on the screen image of the interpreter, even when there was no signed or spoken communication taking place. During the telephone call, when nothing was being said to the Deaf interlocutor, the interpreter took the opportunity to finish his cup of coffee.

(As a footnote, the interpreter contacted the researcher later the same evening to say that he had received a Skype call from the Deaf person asking where the administrator had written the new telephone number. He, the interpreter, had no idea because she had been out of shot. The researcher was able to tell him that she had made a note of it on the back of the original letter. The interpreter said that he would Skype the Deaf participant again to tell him where he could find it.)

Interaction 9 had to be abandoned, not because of picture quality, but because the Deaf interlocutor couldn't quite understand what was meant to happen. The interpreter (D) tried, several times, to interpret the questions about the coffee mornings that were held in a room above the offices but the Deaf person thought that the interpreter, not being in the same room, was speaking to her as herself, rather than as an interpreter. In response to the hearing interlocutor's question about how many people typically attend, the Deaf person signed (to the interpreter) "you know, you've been up there." In response to another interpreted question, the Deaf person simply smiled and waved at the interpreter. The reasons for the breakdown will be examined further in the discussion section below.

Discussion

Although each of the interactions had its own particular features or problems, a pattern did begin to emerge in terms of how the different modes - face-to-face, telephone and remote/video - impacted on alignment and the behaviour of the interpreters.

All three of the face-to-face interactions settled into an approximation of the role-space typical of a collaborative, consultative interaction.

Figure 5: Role-space of a typical collaborative face-to-face interpreted interaction

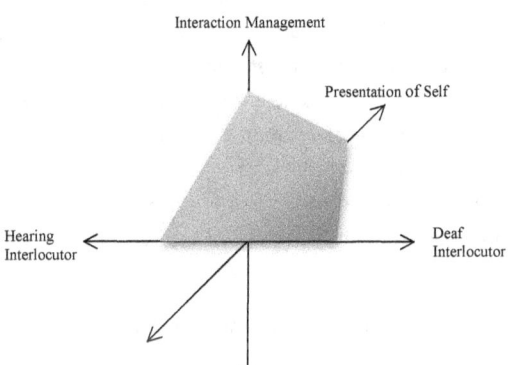

Being relatively informal discussions between interlocutors who either knew each other or/and the interpreters, there was plenty of opportunity for the interpreters to align equally with both interlocutors (the X axis). In interaction 1, the interpreter's deliberate sociolinguistic alignment, or accommodation convergence (Giles, et al., 1991), with the young student appeared to give him the confidence to contribute more freely and fully, as was noted from the change in his body attitude and relaxed use of visual, as well as spoken, feedback. That all three interpreters chose to sit so that they were equidistant from the interlocutors meant that all participants could see each other easily and this clearly contributed to the opportunity for equal and shared alignment. The discussions with the interlocutors after each interaction confirmed that they had felt able to engage with each other and, from an observer's viewpoint, they were clearly creating a shared understanding or 'situation'. This positioning, it should be noted, is entirely contrary to that suggested by some of the signed-language interpreting text books (e.g. Stewart et al., 2004), and the experience of the 'defendant' who took part in the Lessius University/AVIDICUS project (quoted above) only reinforces the necessity for all of the participants to be able to see each other if they are going to be able to take part, comfortably, in a truly dialogical interaction.

This awareness of each other and the availability of visual as well as verbal feedback also allowed the interpreters to use more covert management strategies and it is significant that in two of the interactions, the exchange of glances meant that the interpreters could cope, quite comfortably, with a degree of overlapping-talk. This is, again, an important feature of dialogical interactions and contributes to the creation of a shared 'situation' (see, for example, Garrod and Pickering, 2007). In Interaction 2, by anticipating the end of the previous turn and starting to speak before the interpretation had finished, the hearing interlocutor (social worker) was demonstrating that she was involved in the co-creation of meaning with her co-interlocutor. The fact that the interpreters, through their own back-channelling behaviours, were participating in the creation of the jointly-constructed meaning lends credence to and supports Bélenger's (2004) model of interpreted dialogical interactions.

Figure 4: Bélanger's model of an interpreted dialogical interaction (2004)

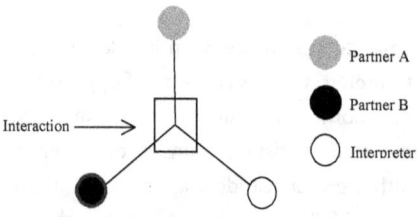

Llewellyn-Jones and Lee (in press) discuss how interpreted telephone interactions demand different points along all three axes. A much greater degree of interaction management is required and, as one of the interlocutors cannot be seen nor see the visual feedback cues that contribute so much to face-to-face interactions, that management has to be overt (rather than covert) and this, in turn, requires more presentation of self on the part of the interpreter as telephone protocols demand verbal feedback cues (and these, of necessity, are authored by the interpreter rather than the Deaf interlocutor).

It should, of course, be remembered that role-spaces are not fixed; instead they develop as the interaction develops, constantly changing to reflect the movement along the axes at different points to reflect the shifts in turns and footing. In each of the three face-to-face interactions, it would be possible to plot how the shapes evolved but, providing the aims of the interlocutors remain unchanged and the focus of the communication doesn't shift, for example from collaborative to confrontational, the generalised space can be predicted and this, then, can be used to predict the most appropriate interactional approach for the interpreter.

Of interest is that in Interaction 2, the face-to-face meeting between the Deaf director and the social worker, the interpreter (B) started in reported speech and only moved to direct speech once she could be sure that both interlocutors would understand the interpreting protocol of using first person.

Ann Corsellis (2008), in her guide for Public Service interpreters, advises that:

> Interpreters may [...] propose that everyone uses direct speech or, because not many people understand what direct speech is, may gently nudge their clients into it after the start of the conversation, by saying something like: 'We will find it easier of you talk to each other directly, instead of to me. Just say, "I am glad to meet you", rather than "Tell her I am glad to meet her" and I will interpret.' If the participants persist in addressing the interpreter, rather than each other, it is often useful for the interpreter simply to look down at their notepad to avoid eye contact, so that the principal participants have to look at each other.
>
> (Corsellis, 2008: 47)

It should be noted that the above advice is intended for interpreters in face-to-face settings. Acceptance of a person speaking in first-person (direct speech) for someone else requires a degree of 'suspension of disbelief' and while it is true that direct speech is usual in such contexts as international meetings, it is expected that those relying on interpretation in these settings are sophisticated enough to understand that this is the norm. It appears somewhat naïve to expect that all participants in interactions will understand that this is how interpreters typically work. That it can lead to confusion was demonstrated in interaction 8. When the interpreter (D) asked the Deaf participant how many people typically attend the coffee mornings, she interpreted in first-person. Those who know that, in signed languages, verbs are typically directional will understand why the Deaf person was confused when she saw "(I'm asking you) how many people attend ... etc." As the Deaf participant was concentrating on the screen, she obviously wasn't aware that the question was actually asked by a hearing person sitting next to her and, it should be remembered, this is hardly a naïve person as she regularly uses interpreters in face-to-face settings such as meetings, medical appointments, etc. It would appear that not being able to see one of the participants is a barrier to understanding everything that is happening.

The most successful telephone call in the recorded data was that made by the administrator to the Pensions Service in interaction 8. She wasn't, of course, interpreting but, rather than announce that it was an interpreted call and expect the recipient to understand the process, she spoke as herself and, using reported speech when she spoke for the Deaf person, explained the process as the interaction unfolded.

In the two remote interpreted interactions that were more successful in terms of their outcomes, the major problems appeared to arise, again, from the interpreter not being able to see all of the interlocutors and the interlocutors either not being able to see the interpreter or one of the other interlocutors. The interpreter in interaction 7 found it difficult to 'design' his spoken renditions because he couldn't see the body language or expressions of the hearing interlocutor. The hearing interlocutor in the same interaction also reported that the conversation had been problematic (and that she had felt "left out") because she couldn't see the interpreter. The Deaf interlocutor in Interaction 8 wasn't aware of what the administrator was doing (or where, indeed, she had written the telephone number) because he couldn't take his eyes off the screen in case he missed something and the Deaf person in Interaction 9 couldn't understand that the question wasn't coming from the interpreter because she, too, was unaware of what was going on around her. In this respect, this small-scale study reflects the findings of the AVIDICUS research teams. The report of the Lessius University findings noted that:

> Whenever there is a screen in a room, people seem to become mesmerised by it. Even when other people are present, a screen grabs the attention, at the expense and to the detriment of personal rapport.
>
> (Balogh and Hertog, 2012)

The Deaf participant in interaction 8 suggested, during the post-recording discussion, that the problem might be solved if the screen showed the other interlocutors as well as the interpreter but the AVIDICUS and New South Wales findings reported earlier in this chapter seem to suggest that this isn't necessarily the answer. In the remote and videoconference interactions studied by those research teams, the screens showed multiple images but, particularly in the New South Wales study, the interlocutors couldn't concentrate on these multiple images simultaneously (Napier, 2011).

Figure 5: Screen shot from the New South Wales study - Scenario 2: (Judge top of screen; Deaf 'defendant' bottom left; remote interpreter bottom right)

Both the interpreter and the Deaf person playing the defendant in the scenario above reiterated the problems caused by not being able to see all of the interlocutors (see their full quotations on pages 4 and 5 above) but it is also noticeable that, particularly in the police interviews filmed by the AVIDICUS Surrey University research team (Braun and Taylor, 2011) even when the interlocutors are shown, all of them were looking at their screens rather than at each other. Consequently none of the interlocutors are actually making eye contact which precludes the natural exchange of glances that allow the joint construction of meaning.

The danger of them not looking at the screens and actually addressing a fellow interlocutor in person was highlighted by Napier in another analysis of the NSW research.

> In this scenario, when the deaf person was answering a question he looked to the judge who had asked him the question. During his response the interpreter needed to request a repetition of a fingerspelled item, but she could not get the client's attention, as he was not looking at the screen on the wall of the courtroom. It took her several attempts to get his attention and then ask the question. By that time, a lot of information had not been interpreted, as the

interpreter was focused on trying to get his attention. Once the defendant realised, he quickly clarified and continued, but had to go back and reiterate what he had already said.

(Napier, 2013)

The effect of remote interpreting on the interpreter's Role-space

It would appear from the remote interpreted interactions recorded with the help of Signing Network and LDAG that the lack of direct contact with one or more of the interlocutors precludes the interpreter from establishing the equality of alignment necessary for the joint construction of meaning (the psycholinguists' situation) which is an essential part of dialogical interactions. The three-dimensional role-shape generated shows this imbalance very clearly.

Figure 6: The role-space of a remote-interpreted interaction

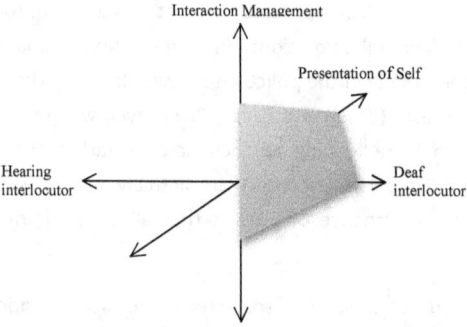

The impact on the axis of interaction management is also shown by the examples from Napier's 2013 analysis of the New South Wales research.

Seen through the lens of Belanger's model of interpreted dialogical interactions (Figure 2), it is clear that rather than helping to create a dialogue, the lack of equal alignment with the interlocutors forces the interpreter into treating the participants contributions as 'talk as text' rather than situated sense making. In other words, the interpreter has no option but to take a monological approach.

Figure 7: A monological 'talk as text' interpreted interaction (after Belanger 2004)

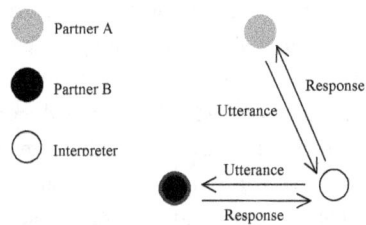

Belanger herself argues that any triangular model of the interpreting process implies a monological approach and that this is highlighted by the inclusion of arrows which suggest that all of the utterances are causal and only made in response to the preceding utterances. As such it is an approach that precludes the joint construction of meaning that is seen as an important feature of interpreted face-to-face interactions (see, for example, Hale, 2007; Roy, 2000; Wadensjö, 1998).

Concluding remarks

The data for the above observations were real-life, spontaneous interactions with outcomes that were important to those involved. Consequently the interlocutors and interpreters were motivated to ensure that, as interactions, they were 'successful', i.e. That the goals of at least some of the interlocutors were met. This type of qualitative, ethnographic/observational research, whilst perhaps not leading to obvious generalisations, is a valuable research method (Hale and Napier, in press) because it is likely to give insights into issues that may well not arise in more controlled qualitative experiments.

These observations could certainly be a catalyst for further discussion on how remote interpreting can be organised so that it is possible for interpreters and interlocutors to engage in truly dialogic interactions when one or more of the participants is in a remote location. Apart from the obvious need for the interpreter to see all of the interlocutors, it would appear that, somehow, the technology needs to allow the participants to make eye contact and be able to catch (in their peripheral vision?) the visual feedback that they miss when communicating via the equipment currently available.

This might also, perhaps, act as a warning against the increasing replacement of traditional, face-to-face interpreting provision that seems to be motivated, in most instances, by nothing more than cost-cutting. In parts of the UK there are already plans to replace 'live' interpreters with remote interpreting services in, for example, front-line medical settings. (On a personal note, the problems encountered in the remotely interpreted interactions staged in Leicester and reported on above, where the participants were known to each other, the interpreters fully qualified, experienced and familiar with the interlocutors, and the repercussions of misunderstandings relatively minor and repairable, would not fill me with confidence if I had to rely on remote services - with unknown interpreters - in a serious or complex medical consultation.)

All of the major advances in the training of community-based interpreters over the past ten or more years have been influenced by the recognition that, in face-to-face interactions, interpreters are real participants who engender trust and confidence in the interlocutors by behaving as people rather than as mere conduits for language transference. Whilst remote interpreting is obviously a valuable tool in the provision of interpreting services, one of the dangers of its indiscriminate use could be that the interpreters are seen, yet again, as mere conduits with the result that Deaf people will rarely experience truly dialogical interactions with members of the wider community.

Acknowledgements

Thanks are due to the Directors of LDAG and its 'Open House' drop-in centre service users for their enthusiastic cooperation and also to the Directors of Signing Network for volunteering to participate in the data collection.

I am also grateful to Jemina Napier for permission to use her screen shots in this paper and the powerpoint presentation at the conference itself, and also for giving me access to her two most recent analyses of the New South Wales remote interpreting research.

References

Association of Sign Language Interpreters; http://www.asli.org.uk/asli-position-statement-on-video-relay-vr-services-p432.aspx. (Last accessed 29.08.2013)

Balogh, K. And Hertog, E. (2011) 'AVIDICUS comparative studies – part II: Traditional, videoconference and remote interpreting in police interviews'. In S. Braun and J. L. Taylor (eds.) Pp117-136.

Bélanger, D-C. (2004) 'Interactional patterns in dialogue interpreting', Journal of Interpretation, 1-18.

Braun, S. And Taylor, J. L. (2011) 'AVIDICUS comparative studies – part I: Traditional interpreting and remote interpreting in police interviews'. In S. Braun and J. L. Taylor (eds.) Pp 85-100.

Braun, S. And Taylor, J. L. (eds.) (2011) Videoconference and Remote Interpreting in Criminal Proceedings. Guildford: University of Surrey

Corsellis, A. (2008) Public Service Interpreting: The First Steps. Basingstoke: Palgrave Macmillan.

Garrod, S. And Pickering, M. J. (2007) 'Alignment in dialogue', in M. G. Gaskell (ed), The Oxford Handbook of Psycholinguistics. Oxford and New York: Oxford University Press, pp. 443-451.

Giles, H., Coupland, N. And Coupland, J. (1991) 'Accommodation theory: communication, context, and consequence', in H. Giles, J. Coupland and N. Coupland (eds.), Contexts of Accommodation. Cambridge and New York: Cambridge University Press, pp. 1-68.

Goffman, E. (1990) The Presentation of Self in Everyday Life. London: Penguin.

Hale, S. B. (2007) Community interpreting. Basingstoke: Palgrave Macmillan.

Hale, S. And Napier, J. (in press) Research Methods in Interpreting: A Practical Resource, London: Bloomsbury.

Llewellyn-Jones, P. And Lee, R. G. (in press) Defining the Role of the Community Interpreter: The Concept of Role-space. Lincoln: SLI Publications.

Miler-Cassino, J. And Rybińska, Z. (2011) 'AVIDICUS comparative studies – part III: Traditional interpreting and videoconference interpreting in prosecution interviews'. In S. Braun and J. L. Taylor (eds.) Pp. 117-136.

Napier, J. (2011) 'Here or there? An assessment of video remote signed language interpreter mediated interaction in court'. In S. Braun and J. L. Taylor (eds.) Pp. 117-136.

Napier, J. (2013).' "You get that vibe": A pragmatic analysis of clarification and communicative accommodation in legal video remote interpreting'. In Meurant, L., Sinte, A., Van Herreweghe, M. & Vermeerbergen, M. (eds.) Sign language research uses and practices: Crossing views on theoretical and applied sign language linguistics (pp.85-110). Nijmegen, The Netherlands: De Gruyter Mouton and Ishara Press.

Roy, C. B. (2000) Interpreting as a Discourse Process. New York and Oxford: Oxford University Press.

Stewart, D. A., Schein J. D. And Cartwright B. E. (2004) Sign Language Interpreting: Exploring its Art and Science. Boston: Pearson/Allyn and Bacon.

Wadensjö, C. (1998) Interpreting as Interaction. London: Longman.

Warnicke, C. And Plejert, C. (2012) 'Turn-organisation in mediated phone interaction using Video Relay Service (VRS)', Journal of Pragmatics 44, 1313-1334.

Knut Weinmeister and Lea Schramm (Germany): The signing questions and answer tool sqat – a tool for translation from written language into sign language and vice versa

Knut Weinmeister is co-founder and co-CEO of Gebärdenwerk, a company located in Hamburg, Germany, which specialises in the translation of written texts into sign language films. Besides holding a first state exam in special education with the education of hearing impaired students and sign language as focal topics, he is also one of the select qualified Deaf interpreters in Germany holding a state certificate in Sign Language Interpreting. Furthermore, he is an experienced translator working from written German into German Sign Language and part of the SQAT translation team.

Lea Schramm holds a B.A. in English Language & Linguistics and Music, an M.A. in Bilingual Translation and a B.A. in Sign Language Interpreting. Having previously worked as an editor for a translation company in the UK with English and German as working languages, she is now part of the team of interpreters at Gebärdenwerk where she produces translations from German Sign Language into written German as part of the SQAT translation team, as well as carrying out content reviews of translations from written German into German Sign Language.

Contact details for correspondence:
knut.weinmeister@gebaerdenwerk.de and lea.schramm@gebaerdenwerk.de

Abstract : It is common knowledge that appropriate technological equipment is required for remote interpreting events such as VRI / VRS. However, technology is also of benefit when producing pre-recorded translations from and into sign language, as exemplified by the Signing Question and Answer Tool SQAT. SQAT provides a translation service between written German and German Sign Language which enables website owners and their Deaf users to communicate without linguistic barriers, with each participant using their preferred language. Deaf users record their message in sign language via webcam and send it to the SQAT translation team. The SQAT team translates the message into written German and sends it to the owner of the website, who writes up their reply and sends it back to the SQAT team. The team then translates the reply into sign language and sends it as a video to the Deaf user.

Thus, SQAT is a communication tool equivalent to online contact forms or e-mail correspondence used by hearing people. In all of these cases, communication takes place not only across a physical distance like with VRI / VRS, but also across a time distance. While written texts denote time distance through the use of certain linguistic features, sign language has so far typically been used in live conversation and up to now there has been little research on the topic of sign language as a language of distance. This creates a challenge for translators when aiming to produce an adequate translation which honours the source and the target languages equally. The SQAT translation team of Deaf and Hearing interpreters has been discussing these and other issues arising from this novel situation and we would like to share with you a couple of suggestions on how to tackle them.

The Signing Question and Answer Tool SQAT –
A tool for translation from written language into sign language and vice versa

1. Outline of SQAT

1.1. VRI / VRS vs. SQAT

The continuous development of modern technology has made it possible to carry out interpreting assignments over a distance, with the interpreter not being physically present in the same location as the Deaf and Hearing clients. Such is the case with video remote interpreting (VRI) and video relay services (VRS) where the interpreter uses technological equipment such as a computer, a headset, a webcam or a videophone to access the conversation remotely. However, technology does not only support live interpreting settings, but it can also be of benefit for the production of translations from and into video-recorded sign language texts.

In addition to the physical distance of the interpreter or translator, respectively, as in a remote interpreting situation, the translation setting is in addition characterised by the time distance which passes between the production of the source text, the reception of the source text by the translator, the production of the target text by the translator, and the reception of the target text by the target audience. This form of communication over a place and time distance entails certain challenges for translators, as shall be addressed in more detail in the following sections of this paper. In order to understand these challenges better, it is useful to describe how Deaf and Hearing people communicate with each other over a physical distance.

1.2. Communication over a distance

Hearing people communicating with other hearing people have various choices of technological equipment for communication over a distance. They can use the telephone to make phone calls, send e-mails or text messages to each other or use online contact forms to get in touch, e.g. For contacting the owner of an internet website.

Deaf people, on the contrary, are much more restricted in their choice of communication technology when wanting to contact Hearing people, if they want to use sign language. While Deaf people can use VRI / VRS in some countries as a functionally equivalent tool to the telephone used by Hearing people, when it comes to writing e-mails or using online contact forms, they need to revert to written language. They can, of course, ask a Hearing person for assistance, e.g. To correct their written text or to make / interpret phone calls. However, in all of these cases, it would be the responsibility of the Deaf person to organise everything themselves and, depending on the circumstances, pay for the service given. There is no standardised technical solution which Deaf people can use for this way of communication. Thus, the effort for Deaf people is disproportionately higher than for hearing people. Considering that functionally equivalent access to telecommunication services is defined as a civil right in the US[6], this is quite a shocking situation.

This is where the Signing Question and Answer Tool SQAT comes in. A communication tool equivalent to the online contact forms or e-mail correspondence used by Hearing people, the aim of SQAT is to give Deaf people more access to communication with Hearing people while still using sign language as their language of choice. SQAT provides the organisational and structural framework for successful communication, and furthermore, the SQAT service is free for Deaf people to use.

1.3. What is SQAT?

The Signing Question and Answer Tool SQAT, which was created by the German company Gebärdenwerk, is a tool for translation from written language into sign language and vice versa. The SQAT translation service provides a translation service between written German and German Sign Language which enables website owners and their Deaf users to communicate without linguistic barriers, with each participant using their preferred language.

Qualified Hearing and Deaf interpreters work together in the SQAT translation team. The translations are produced by a native speakers or signer, respectively, of Language A, and subsequently checked for correctness and completeness by a native speaker or signer of Language B. The 'tandems' which are made up of a Deaf and a Hearing interpreter each and the 'four-eyes principle' are thus vital components of the SQAT translation service which help to maintain high standards of quality when producing translations.

As has been previously mentioned, the aim of SQAT is to provide Deaf people with a communication option equivalent to of the written e-mails or online contact forms used by Hearing people. Therefore, SQAT does not replace the use of an interpreter for settings addressing personal or sensitive topics, or for expert discussions. Rather,

SQAT is used for general questions, for arranging an appointment or for making other preliminary arrangements between conversational partners – thus, for the same contents that e-mails or contact forms are used by Hearing people. In this way, SQAT helps to avoid misunderstandings or insecurities which can arise in written communication between Deaf and Hearing people. Writing is often characterised by communicative difficulties as it forces Deaf people to use a foreign language of communication.

The UN Convention on the Rights of Persons with Disabilities deals with disabled peoples' rights to freedom of expression and opinion, and access to information in Article 21. In this Article, State Parties are asked to accept, facilitate, recognise and promote the use of sign language. In addition, the Behindertengleichstellungsgesetz (BGG) [law against the discrimination of disabled people] which was passed in Germany in 2002 states in § 9 the right of Deaf people to use sign language when communicating with public authorities. SQAT complies both with the UN Convention and with the BGG. SQAT provides for effective communication between Deaf and Hearing people and makes communication at eye level possible. Each participant can use their preferred language, creating a smooth flow of communication. It also provides Deaf people with a better access to a two-way information flow. This principle, enabling Deaf people to actively submit messages themselves rather than just consuming information in a passive way, complies with the philosophy of the Web 2.0.

1.4. How does SQAT work?

A SQAT translation cycle consists of the following five steps:

1. The Deaf person signs a message, for example, a question regarding the information on a website, in sign language. They record their signed message on video via webcam and send it to the SQAT service via Internet.

2. The SQAT translation team receives the Deaf person's video and translates its contents from sign language into written language. After the translation has been checked, the written message is forwarded via e-mail to the Hearing addressee, who has implemented the SQAT service on their website.

3. The Hearing addressee receives the written message. They reply to it in writing and send their reply to the SQAT service via e-mail.

4. The SQAT service receives the written reply, translate it into sign language and record it on video. After the translation has been checked, it is sent to the Deaf person.

5. The Deaf person receives the reply to their question as well as a link to an overview of the personal SQAT history regarding their question.

This five-step process making up a SQAT cycle is illustrated by the following figure:

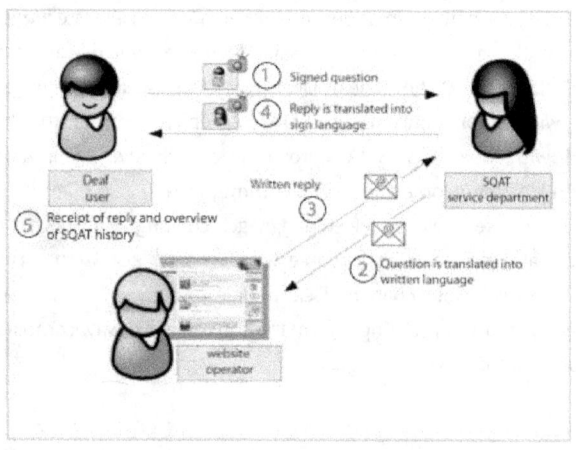

Figure 1: The SQAT cycle

1.5. Where is SQAT used?

In 2011, the German government passed a legislation for barrier-free information technology (BITV 2.0), which includes some regulations on providing online contents in sign language. SQAT helps to fulfil the aim of this legislation and has been embedded on websites from various areas. Federal Ministries in Germany, such as the Federal Ministry of Finance and the Federal Ministry of Transport, Building and Urban Development, offer the SQAT service on their websites. The Federal Chancellor and the Federal Government have also embedded SQAT on their websites, as has the Federal Anti-Discrimination Agency. Another client using SQAT is the parcel delivery service DHL. Also, the Swiss Post makes use of the SQAT service.

2. Translation challenges

2.1 Live conversation vs. Time-delayed conversation

While SQAT has many advantages, as has been discussed above, it also presents translators with additional challenges and difficulties due to the specific communication conditions arising from its given framework. In the case of SQAT, communication takes place not only across a physical distance like with VRI / VRS, but also across a time distance. Sign language as used by Deaf people so far is typically used in live conversations and in a direct dialogue between two or more people talking to each other at the same point in time. Therefore, immediate communicative feedback between signers is possible and is provided.

However, the translation situation with SQAT is different: There is a time delay between production and reception of messages in the conversation. Therefore, the distinct message sent by each conversational partner resembles, in itself, a monologue rather than a dialogue. As a result, immediate feedback is not possible. This may be a challenge for translators if, for example, contents of a signed message are difficult to understand due to poor recording quality, or the content within a message is ambiguous or unclear. Unlike in most live (community) interpreting situations, translators cannot ask for clarification straight away.

2.2 Signed vs. Written modality

The act of signing, like the act of speaking, is by its nature transient unless it is recorded in some form, e.g. via video technology. Its production mostly takes place spontaneously and any language production errors are corrected by the producer or the receiver during the conversation, as they occur.

Written language, on the contrary, is fixed and a written text is the result of a planned process, in which the text produced can be corrected several times before it is given to its readers. This means that signed and written texts differ in the ways in which they are composed. Therefore, as in the case of SQAT, the translation between two languages using different modalities is an additional challenge for translators.

2.3 Language of proximity vs. Language of distance

The time and modality factors above result in a different way how signed and written texts are structured and what types of language they use. Here it is helpful to draw on Hansen's distinction between language of proximity and language of distance.

Typically, language of proximity is connected with the concept of speaking and is characterised, for example, by privateness, familiarity of communication partners, physical proximity and referencing to the here and now[7]. Language of proximity shows a low degree of planning, resulting in linear progression between stretches of text such as the connective 'and then' in German[8]. Also, the people communicating have a shared knowledge of the situation, which is why there is, for instance, no need for explicit lexical naming of reference objects[9].

Language of distance, on the other hand, is connected with the concept of writing and is characterised, for for example, by publicness, unfamiliarity of communication partners, physical distance, and lack of referencing to the here and now[10]. Language of distance shows a more hierarchical and complex structure with texts using connectives such as 'while' and 'finally' in German[11]. Reference objects need to be identified unambiguously[12].

Up into the 1980s, sign language was mostly used in situations which required the physical proximity of conversation partners due to the lack of an established writing

---

7	Hansen 2012: 213-214
8	ibid.: 215
9	ibid.: 216
10	ibid.: 213
11	ibid.: 215
12	ibid.: 217

system for sign languages[13]. In addition, sign languages were hardly recognised and therefore mostly used in informal situations, such as in Deaf clubs, Deaf families or Deaf schools[14]. These linguistic conditions mean that signed texts mostly display characteristics of language of proximity[15].[16]

However, the fact that SQAT is equivalent to written correspondence such as e-mails means that its external factors ask for a language of distance to be used. The question is whether, and if so, where a pre-recorded signed text fits into this characterisation of proximity and distance. For German Sign Language, there is no research yet regarding the systematic comparison of syntactic constructions of a spontaneous, unplanned discourse with texts that use language of distance[17]. Also, little research has been carried out on videotaped (and thus fixed) texts in a signed modality, and not much is known about the linguistic properties of fixed signed texts. Whereas the discipline of sight interpreting deals with the translation of fixed written texts into sign language, the sign language in sight interpreting is produced live and not recorded. Also, spoken language in sight interpreting is produced live and not written down in form of a fixed text.

3. Tackling the challenge

Faced with this challenge, the Deaf and Hearing interpreters of the SQAT translation team have been discussing these and other issues arising from this novel situation together and collected some ideas on how to tackle them. The situation outlined above creates a challenge for translators when aiming to produce an adequate translation which honours the source and the target languages equally.

It is also important in this matter to maintain a balance between a translation which is too literal and translation which is too free. At the same time, the situational context has to be taken into account for each individual translation and influences

---

13   ibid.: 224
14   ibid.
15   ibid.
16   Although sign languages do not have an established written form, they can still use language of distance – this is the case with sign language stories, poetry and jokes, which are planned, monologic texts with a fixed topic (Hansen 2012: 218-220).
17   Hansen 2012: 221

the translator's choices; thus, the same source text can call for different translations according to the target situation and the target addressees[18].

Therefore, it is unrealistic to establish one and the same translation rule applicable for all cases. However, a set of agreed norms will be helpful for translators in order to have some guidelines they can refer to.

3.1 Some translation guidelines

The SQAT team has been drafting some translation guidelines following the criteria mentioned previously. They concern typical introductory and concluding formulations as well as the structure of written texts typically occurring in the context of SQAT.

An example could be a Deaf person asking the DHL parcel service the following fictitious short question about a parcel they are expecting. The table below shows a gloss transcription of the question asked as well as a suggested translation into written language:

Signed question in English (and German) glosses	Translation
HELLO, MY NAME JANE SMITH. MY PARCEL RECEIVE WHEN? ME WAIT++. BYE. HALLO, MEIN NAME JANE SMITH. MEIN PAKET BEKOMMEN WANN? ICH WARTEN++. TSCHÜS.	Hello, I have been waiting for my parcel for a while and was wondering when I will receive it? Yours sincerely, Jane Smith Hallo, Ich warte schon länger auf mein Paket und wollte fragen, wann ich es bekomme? Mit freundlichen Grüßen, Jane Smith

Table 1: Sample question with a translation suggestion

---

18   Snell-Hornby, 1999: 145

As can be seen, in this case it was decided to translate the introductory sign HELLO (HALLO) one-to-one into written language, using "hello" ("hallo") instead of "Dear Sir or Madam" ("Sehr geehrte Damen und Herren") or a similar phrase. The reason for this is that Hearing people using a contact form or e-mail to get in touch with the DHL often would use "hello" as well to begin their written message. However, in a different context where it would be more appropriate to use a more formal phrase in written German, the translation may differ and also use a more formal expression.

The text was also re-structured partly for the translation: While the name in the signed question was given at the beginning, it was decided for the translation to move the name of the person asking the question to the very end, as it would be customary in a written e-mail.

Finally, the closing phrase BYE was translated as "Yours sincerely" ("Mit freundlichen Grüßen"), since this is the common way to conclude a written letter or e-mail.

The following table shows a fictitious written reply by DHL to the Deaf person as well as a suggested translation of the reply as glosses:

Written reply	Translation in English (and German) glosses
Dear Ms Smith, Many thanks for your query. We posted your parcel yesterday. Yours sincerely, DHL Paket Customer service	DEAR MS SMITH, ME WHO? THIS-IS DHL PAKET ITS CUSTOMER SERVICE. YOU BEEN QUESTION CONCERNING PARCEL WHERE? QUESTION. THANK-YOU. YESTERDAY WE BEEN SENDING YOUR PARCEL. BYE.
Sehr geehrte Frau Smith, Vielen Dank für Ihre Anfrage. Wir haben Ihr Paket gestern an Sie versendet. Mit freundlichen Grüßen, Kundenservice DHL Paket	SEHR GEEHRTE FRAU SMITH, ICH WER? DAS-IST DHL PAKET SEIN KUNDENSERVICE. DU GEWESEN FRAGE ZUSAMMENHANG PAKET WO? FRAGE, DANKE. GESTERN WIR GEWESEN DEIN PAKET SCHICKEN. TSCHÜS.

Table 2: Sample reply with a translation suggestion

For the translation from German Sign Language into written German, it was decided to transfer the opening phrase "Dear Ms Smith" ("Sehr geehrte Frau Smith") one-to-one to the translation because it can be assumed that the Deaf person is familiar with the standard opening phrase of letters in German ("Sehr geehrte/r Herr/Frau ...") and would expect the reply to begin with this phrase. This was deemed acceptable by the Deaf native speakers in the SQAT translation team.

In this translation, the text was slightly restructured insofar that the person replying – in this case, DHL Paket Customer service) was mentioned at the beginning of the translation since it is more typical in German Sign Language to introduce the protagonist at the beginning.

The closing phrase "Yours sincerely" ("Mit freundlichen Grüßen") was, unlike the opening phrase, not adopted one-to-one in the translation. The reason for this is that this formulation looked cumbersome and unnatural in the Deaf team members' eyes and the closing phrase BYE (TSCHÜSS) was more appropriate in the given context.

The issues mentioned in the fictitious examples above are based on translation guidelines drafted by the SQAT team which are listed as an overview in the two following tables.

German Sign Language (DGS)	Written German
HELLO / GOOD MORNING / GOOD AFTERNOON / DEAR ... (HALLO / GUTEN TAG / SEHR GEEHRTE(R) ...)	Follow DGS, but keep in mind the addressee (target audience)
Introductory sentence: MY NAME [fingerspelling] (Einleitung: MEIN NAME [Fingeralphabet])	Closing sentence: Yours sincerely, [fingerspelling] (Verabschiedung: Mit freundlichen Grüßen, [Fingeralphabet])
BYE (TSCHÜS)	Yours sincerely, [Name] (Mit freundlichen Grüßen, [Name])
No closing sentence	Generally no closing sentence, no name

Table 3: Some translation guidelines – German Sign Language into written German

Written German	German Sign Language (DGS)
Hello / Good morning / afternoon / Dear / Dear Sir or Madam (Hallo / Guten Tag / Sehr geehrte(r) ... / Sehr geehrte Damen und Herren)	Follow written German text
Yours sincerely, (Mit freundlichen Grüßen,)	BYE (TSCHÜS)
Closing sentence: [Name and position]	Introductory sentence: [Name and position]

Table 4: Some translation guidelines – Written German into German Sign Language

4. Outlook

With the increasing recognition of sign languages as complete and self-contained languages, they are used more and more in formal situations, for example by Deaf academics giving presentations in sign language[19]. Therefore, sign languages are no longer restricted to be used for personal and direct communication in informal situations only and have to find or develop adequate ways of expression for the new purposes they are used for[20]. Sign languages are in a similar situation as French, Italian and German were in the 13th to 16th century: Back then, only Latin was deemed adequate for academic, theological and philosophic texts[21]. Lacking alternatives, text patterns as well as grammar-related points were copied from Latin to these popular languages[22].

Hansen[23] rightly claims that systematic research regarding the use of language of proximity versus language of distance in sign languages is yet to be carried out. Specifically, research for more detailed guidelines for translation is needed, for example, for sign language texts translated into a written letter, an e-mail or into other forms of written text.

---

[19] Hansen 2012: 213
[20] ibid.
[21] ibid.
[22] ibid.
[23] ibid.: 218

5. Bibliography

Gesetz zur Gleichstellung behinderter Menschen (Behindertengleichstellungsgesetz – BGG), http://www.gesetze-im-internet.de/bgg/BJNR146800002.html (accessed on 25 August 2013)

Hansen, Martje: Textlinguistik: Gebärdensprache im Kontext. In: Eichmann, Hanna, Hansen, Martje and Heßmann, Jens (eds.) (2012) Handbuch Deutsche Gebärdensprache – Sprachwissenschaftliche und anwendungsbezogene Perspektiven, Seedorf: Signum Verlag.

Haualand, Hilde (2010): Provision of Videophones and Video Interpreting for the Deaf and Hard of Hearing – A Comparative Study of Video Interpreting (IV) Systems in the US, Norway and Sweden, The Swedish Institute of Assistive Technology (SIAT) (Hjälpmedelsinstitutet, HI) and Fafo Institute for Labour and Social Research, Vällingby.

Snell-Hornby, Mary, Hönig, Hans G., Kußmaul, Paul, Schmitt, Peter A. (eds.) (1999): Handbuch Translation, Tübingen: Stauffenburg Verlag.

SQAT website: http://www.sqat.eu

UN Convention on the Rights of People with Disabilities, http://www.un.org/disabilities/convention/conventionfull.shtml (accessed on 25 August 2013)

Verordnung zur Schaffung barrierefreier Informationstechnik nach dem Behindertengleichstellungsgesetz (Barrierefreie-Informationstechnik-Verordnung - BITV 2.0), http://www.gesetze-im-internet.de/bitv_2_0/BJNR184300011.html (accessed on 25 August 2013)

Roger Beeson, David Wolfenden, Mo Bergson and Christopher Stone (UK): Modern technology and modern interpreter

Roger Beeson has been a freelance BSL interpreter for 18 years, having qualified in 1988 whilst working as a Teacher of the Deaf. He co-founded and still co-owns the independent e-newsli e-group. He established and ran the Healthy Deaf Minds meetings in London until they became Deaf-run. He is Chair of Trustees of RAD, Sonus (formerly Hampshire Deaf Association) and Deafinitely Theatre. Despite being of retirement age he continues to be a general purpose BSL interpreter, still learning on the job.

David Wolfenden has been interpreting for 23 years and is currently employed with the National Deaf Child & Adolescent Mental Health Service in Taunton, Somerset. He is a trained Mentor and Assessor of candidates to the interpreting profession, David also retains an active role in the professional association having been involved in the governance of ASLI for many years. He also teaches on various Interpreter Training Programmes throughout the UK.

Mo Bergson has worked as a freelance Sign Language Interpreter in the south of England for over 25 years. Initially qualifying as a Social Worker, and working in this capacity with deaf people, she later retrained as an interpreter gaining Full Registration status in 1995. Whilst employed in a variety of domains, including police work, child protection and therapy she developed an interest in small group situations where the interpersonal dimension has a significant effect on the interpreting dynamic. She has been involved at various levels of interpreter training and continues to co run workshops for both interpreters and also hearing professionals who work with them. In addition to being part of a peer group she facilitates one for other interpreters and is a one to one mentor.

Christopher Stone trained as a BSL/English interpreter at the Centre for Deaf Studies, University of Bristol 1995-1997 and now works as an interpreter, interpreter trainer and researcher. His phd titled 'Towards a Deaf translation norm' was supervised by Dr Rachel Sutton-Spence and published in 2009 by Gallaudet University Press. His is currently undertaking: a longitudinal study examining predictors for sign language learning and sign language interpreter aptitude. He has also explored (with Robert Adam and Dr Breda Carty) Deaf people working as translators and interpreters within the Deaf community and at the institutional interface. He recently took up a position as Associate Professor, Department of Interpretation, Gallaudet University. He still maintains an interpreting practice within community and conference settings.

Contact details for correspondence: Mo Bergson mobergson@me.com.

Abstract: With an ever increasing number of interpreters with diverse work patterns, areas of work and interests it is now both easier and harder to find ways to get back to the basic CPD of talking to like-minded interpreters to discuss our work. In the 21st century these groups need not be local and this presentation aims to discuss the formation and continuance of a reflective practice group formed by the presenters where technology is use to support and benefit the group.

We intend to show how we can use technology in ways that support us to do basic things such as peer support, looking at our work, reflective practice; talking about the basic job of interpreting while drawing upon different strengths in the group to draw upon theoretical things too.

We will discuss how we formed a group and the initial face-to-face meetings we had. We will discuss the types of discussions that we have, including discussing ethics, filming and giving feedback on our work, the group as an extended de-briefing mechanism, etc. We will include examples of real world usefulness of such a group. (i.e. Rehearsing arguments, rehearsing presentations/training, sharing drafts of articles, moral support during times of need, sharing resource materials, etc.).

Further discussions will take place concerning the ways in which we now use technology to enhance the service we provide to service users in a more environmentally-friendly way and to benefit them by providing a better service.

The members of the group are no longer in the same geographical location and we will go on to discuss how we have maintained our group. This will include examples of the technology employed and the various iterations we've worked though to get to what we have now.

Modern Technology and the Modern Interpreter

We are all modern interpreters. We all use modern technology to support us in our work. As an example of what we mean, who remembers the Facsimile Machine, The Telephone Answering Machine that used cassette tapes, the Typewriter that used Carbon Paper, the Portable Telephone that was as large as a brick, having to look through lots of reference books in order to do preparatory work for your assignments, consulting a paper map that had to be unfolded (and then re-folded) in order to find your way to the assignment venue, the telephone box (famously red in Britain) where you had to have a supply of small change in order to make a call to say you'd be late arriving for the job, or the Filofax with a nice small pen that meant you had finally made it as a professional!

Of course, none of the above are used by interpreters in their practice today. Our assignments automatically transfer themselves to our calendar apps at the click of a button, communication with clients and venue couldn't be easier with mobile and tablet telephony, we are able to conduct detailed preparation for assignments with our sign language users via facetime and skype before the event, our driving and walking directions are highlighted for us as soon as we leave the house and are available in our pockets, showing us where we are in relation to our destination, live, via GPS. All our invoicing is equally seamless when we can now issue a statement at the touch of a button and have our bank account automatically updated when payment has been received. It will even send out reminders to late payers. We can source assignments too via online websites such as BSL Beam (in the UK), and of course, all the documentation we need for an assignment can be selected from multiple online virtual clouds.

Just a quick look around the conference room confirmed that we are even using this modern technology in our everyday lives when watching presentations or taking part in workshops; delegates were taking screen-shots of powerpoint slides and videoing presentations as well as taking detailed notes on their tablets.

As developing professionals, we also use technology to enable us to reflect, monitor, diagnose, assess and supervise one another. We take part in online discussions and peer support groups via web-based applications to ensure that our practice is regularly reviewed and mentoring can take place. By using discrete, unobtrusive video cameras we are able to constantly record and review our work, we can share our very practice with our peers and colleagues via remote discussions online and gain assistance in identifying areas for development.

What we used to have to do was to physically come together in a room, sit around in a circle in uncomfortable chairs, watch a VHS video of our work (that was filmed by a briefcase-sized VHS Camera on a large tripod with large lights plugged into the wall, wires and cables trailing across peoples legs) on a cathode ray television that had to be tuned in to the correct frequency to receive the picture.

Now, of course, things are very much easier, and we would like to focus on our own peer support group as a further example of how technology can support us.

We did indeed begin as a face-to-face group when we were all based in the same city of London. We met on a regular basis to discuss our work, issues and dilemmas, whilst also bringing video files (on memory stick or otherwise) of our work for analysis and comment. We held email discussions between meetings, and shared articles as email attachments. All of this was designed to ensure that we met our Regulatory requirements of undertaking Continuous Professional Development (CPD) activities totaling 35 hours per year.

We began with no fixed format, took notes to reference our discussions, that also served to evidence our CPD. The amount of Modern Technology involved in such a group was considerable:

> Doodle.com to organise the dates for our meetings.
>
> Flipcam to record our work.
>
> Dropbox and email to share resources.
>
> Skype, facetime and other applications to meet virtually.

When we moved away from London, we began to regularly meet remotely and trialled various technologies to see how well they suited our purposes;

Skype, facetime (by ipad and iphone in addition to Macs and pcs) led us to using gotomeeting.com which seemed to give a more stable performance. We had also experimented with google hangout, although we found this sometimes limited our interaction.

What became evident through our experiences was the need for some discipline to our sessions together; Note-Taking, Turn-Taking and Chairing became more important. It also became clear that there are limits to the freeware solutions available on the internet, and of course, no web-based service is going to be effective unless all participants have a high bandwidth connection. Time-delay can be an issue at times, especially when participants are in different countries – but reverting to the 'old fashioned' technology of emails being read by the recipient whilst the sender is fast asleep ensures that, when the time comes to hold an online session, all participants are fully prepared.

The positive consequences of meeting in this way are significant; being remote does help the group to keep their discussion focused. With the requirement for more ground rules and somewhat stricter behavioural expectations, the group has become more formalised. A short intensive session of discussion and information sharing, leaving silence when the connection is ended, does encourage participants to reflect and think more deeply. The ability to use applications such as doodle.com does enable everyone to slot such development opportunities into their working week. It enables and encourages self-development – which is always a good thing in a professional practitioner.

None of the technology we use is scary nor is it difficult to use. We already are, clearly, as a profession, very used to such devices and software. We are Modern Interpreters and we are using Modern Technology to support both our practice and in our Development, no competition required.

Mark Zaurov (Germany): Online interpreting: the advantages of new technologies supporting the needs of interpreters and their customers

Mark Zaurov is an independent scholar and a doctoral candidate at the University of Hamburg. His fields are Deaf Jews in Art, Politics and the Sciences, and the Deaf Holocaust. He published a couple of books and won several fellowships with, for example, Charles H. Revson Foundation, the Center for Advanced Holocaust Studies, United States Holocaust Memorial Museum. He is a nationally certified interpreter of the first generation Deaf interpreters trained at the University of Hamburg and has been working in settings such as international conferences and translation projects. His working languages are German Sign Language, International Signs, and American Sign Language and German.

Contact details for correspondence: mark.zaurov@gmail.com

Abstract: The latest online video communication technologies revolutionised life in the Deaf community by reducing communication barriers. In the USA, the video relay industry has been proliferating. There, it is financed by the government which is not the case in many other countries.

In Germany, more and more Deaf people are self-employed like me. German law restricts the budget of handicapped entrepreneurs compared to those who work under "able" employers providing them with contracts. The lower budget exerts immense economic pressure intensified by interpreters' attitudes towards their honorarium. In this talk I am sharing my experience of working with an interpreter via Skype and point out the benefits entailed both for me and my interpreter. I will also introduce other video relay servies in Germany and their difference to interpreting via Skype.

I would like to encourage a discussion about the reasons why many interpreters hesitate to use this technology and show the need to include new technologies into interpreter training programs in Germany.

The latest online video communication technologies have revolutionised life in the Deaf community by reducing communication barriers. In the USA, the proliferating video relay industry is funded by the government (Federal Communications Commission) via a percentage taken from the telecom end-user revenues. In many other countries, however, similar services can not rely on government funding.

In Germany, the maximum individual budget for interpreters available to deaf citizens twice as high for employees compared to self-employed persons. The number of self-employed persons in Germany is rising, and I am one of them. I have to manage with 550 E per month to cover interpreting costs of 55 E (now up to 75 E) per hour. Interpreting time and travel time are billed with the same hourly rate, expenses are added. For me, this situation was unbearable, and I started to look for interpreters who would make phone calls for me via Skype. This way, I could talk to persons I wanted to contact without having to personally go there and arrange for interpreters who would bill travel time and waiting time in addition to interpreting time. The interpreters I asked were less than enthusiastic about my idea. Certainly, it had to do with the fact that I would only pay them the interpreting time which made the assignment less attractive - since there are more jobs than interpreters can cover, paid travel and waiting were something my assignment could not compete with. None of these factors were mentioned when my interpreters turned down my offer. The main reason was: they refused to even try, claiming that two-dimensionality would hamper the interpreting proccess.

After one interpreter finally agreed to experiment, a wonderful and long-lasting collaboration began. At that time she had just had a baby and liked the idea of working from home. I have been working with this interpreter via Skype in combination with a telephone for many of my conversations over the past six years.

In my view, 2-D was indeed an issue, however something that could be dealt with. We are talking about a visual language with spacial grammar, and in theory the x-z plane would only be represented as a spacial illusion on an x-y plane. However, our habit of watching television and working with computers has made it extremely hard to ignore this illusion. In interpreting education, videos are used for practice.

The argument that representation in 2-D was the key issue of tele-interpreting, was absurd. Our discussion at the EFSLI workshop revealed that this was indeed not the problem. Many comments intended to affirm the challenges of "2-D", actually brought up quite different aspects of tele-interpreting revolving around the loss of context and unfamiliarity with telephone etiquette. The flatness of the screen is something we can not debate or work with until 3-D is introduced on screens for every-day use. The loss of context, however, is something we can deal with. If you do not know what else is happening around the deaf or hearing interlocutor you see on screen, you might lose meaningful context. The participants might also feel uneasy, as if they were losing "touch" and in consequence, mistrust the interpreting process. Misunderstandings can come about because deaf interlocutors are not familiar with telephone etiquette and the hearing interlocutor who is not "facing" the fact that she is talking to someone deaf would not see any reason why "telephone" etiquette might just not apply in this situation.

In Belgium, as one participant pointed out, telephone interpreting is part of interpreter education. Not only should remote-interpreting become part of interpreter training programs but a profound understanding of telephone-etiquette and how to mediate between the two different cultures on the phone and on screen should be acquired in interpreter education everywhere in Europe. In general, we should not conflate the various issues having to do with remote-interpreting as "2-D" but clarify what is really meant in order to be able to benefit from remote-interpreting in the future.

Nicole Montagna (USA): The digital revolution and sign language interpreting, impact and implications

Nicole Montagna is originally from New York City and developed her interpreting career in the San Francisco Bay Area. Her journey into sign language has taken her around the world, including Gallaudet University, two Deaflympics and three WASLI conferences. She has been exploring the impact of the digital revolution on the sign language interpreting profession for the past few years, since her MA studies in Instructional Technologies. Currently, her home base is once again Brooklyn, NY, now with her husband and daughter. When she isn't interpreting, she's doing yoga, editing videos and trying to keep up with techno-trends. Www.interpretopia.net

Contact details for correspondence: interpretopia@gmail.com

Abstract: Throughout history, skepticism towards technological innovations has been a common a pattern. Similarly, concern has been expressed in the interpreting field about "technology" and its impact on our profession, from the delivery of our services, to the possibility of being replaced by it. My paper outlines a history of technological innovations and their impacts on sign language interpreting, from the development of cinema, to video compression. Spanning a century these two major technological feats have had major implications on sign language in general, and interpreting in particular. Cinematic tools, combined with the internet, have expanded the ability to develop sign language fluency, interpreting skills and broaden the scope of delivering interpreting services. I define "modern technology" in terms of digital tools, specifying technologies that we find most concerning, and those from which we benefit. Some of the concerns that have been expressed are related to the feasibility of combining artificial intelligence and machine translation to replace interpreters, efforts that are usually framed as supplemental. Studies referenced are those that explore the application of artificial intelligence and machine translation towards sign language, such as the development of sign language synthesizers, and signing avatars. There are possible ways in which technologies mitigate interpreting for the better, through expanded computer mediated text communication, the ubiquity of cameras in computers and mobile devices, videoconferencing directly with other sign language users, and advancements in captioning. This paper also discusses the convergence of various innovations that have had a positive impact on our field such as, searchable maps, mobile devices, web-based small business apps, and the increased accessibility of extra linguistic information and access to sign language stimuli via the world wide web. Finally, in what ways are our technological challenges unique because of our field, and which are general consequences of a digitised modern society?

Helen Fuller and Brigitte Francois (UK): Technology vs interpreter- support or replacement?

Brigitte Francois BA, pgdiped, RSLI Well known as an International Sign Language interpreter Brigitte has worldwide experience of working as an interpreter in a variety of settings. A pioneer, Brigitte was a founder member of the professional association of Sign Language Interpreters in Belgium, the first sign language interpreter to be registered with the European Commission's Directorate General for Interpretation (SCIC) and founder of Significan't UK Ltd, parent company of signvideo, the UK's leading video relay and remote interpreting service. Brigitte is managing director of Sign Language Interpreting Direct, an agency providing high quality interpreting services to universities and Deaf professionals.

Helen Fuller RSLI, MCMI Working as a BSL/English Interpreter since 1992, Helen qualified in 1996 and has a broad range of interpreting experience. She is a qualified assessor and verifier for vocational qualifications in interpreting and has developed and delivered training for a number of organisations. Working regularly in video relay services for the last 4 years, Helen delivers training for signvideo, the leading VRS service in the UK.

Contact details for correspondence: training@signvideo.co.uk

Abstract: With tales of interpreters taken from the community to work in call centres, being made to make calls with no time allowed for preparation and rumours of some less than ethical behaviour on the part of service providers in the States, it is understandable that interpreters in Europe may have some reservations about the advent of Video Relay Services in the region. We aim to show that, with the right approach, VRS can be the interpreter's and the Deaf community's friend. Using our experience of working in VRS and case studies from the Deaf community we will show how using technology can benefit both the interpreter and the Deaf person, making the most efficient use of limited resources. We will also look at what steps stakeholders need to take to ensure that services are provided in the best way for interpreters and service users (Deaf and hearing).

VRS - Friend or Foe

Introduction

Until recently sign language interpreters had to be co-located with the Deaf party in the interaction that they were interpreting. As a result a large part of the interpreter's day could be spent travelling from one location to another, thus limiting the number of assignments they could undertake in one day. A general shortage of qualified interpreters has also meant that it has been difficult to book an interpreter at short notice. Whilst it was possible to book interpreters for planned meetings and training events, the everyday ad hoc interactions between colleagues by their very nature went uninterpreted leaving the Deaf staff member still isolated from their hearing colleagues and missing out on the opportunity to participate in informal (but often important) workplace communication. One solution is for an interpreter to be booked to be available during the ordinary working day and ready to interpret as an when required. This can prove costly and inefficient as the interpreter may be booked for a seven hour working day and provide interpreting for a small fraction of that time. Whilst it meets the needs of the Deaf person, it can be frustrating and demoralising for the interpreter who finds themselves not using the skills for which they have been hired for long periods throughout the day and who all too often is aware that there are other Deaf people who are not receiving a service as they sit doing nothing.

Internet and data-streaming technology has advanced to the place where it is possible to develop online video communication tools to a level that makes it viable for sign language to be transmitted via the telephone network. As is often the case the technology was not developed with Deaf people in mind. In the same way that text messaging on mobile phones allowed Deaf people to communicate with friends and family without the need of a fixed line and a textphone, video communication software, now freely available, allows Deaf people to communicate with each other but this time in their own language. The opportunity to replace existing text relay services with video relay services, delivering a more functionally equivalent telephone experience for Deaf people has become a real possibility.

Video Relay Services

America lead the way in the development of Video Relay Services in the mid 1990s and a number of different services developed across the States. Initially starting as an adjunct of existing interpreting services the video relay service in America is now mostly controlled by one or two larger companies that have a wide range of interests and no real connection with the community that they serve. As a result of regulatory requirements larger call centres have been established to provide the 24 hour a day, 365 days a year service and the number of qualified interpreters is not sufficient to meet the demand. These service providers recruit trainee interpreters and pay for their training whilst requiring the trainee interpreters to deal with calls. This, despite the fact that the National Consortium of Interpreter Education Centers states that "The highly demanding and complex work of the video interpreter requires experience and skill" [1]. Comments on an article on Street Leverage, a community blog for sign language interpreters, indicate that the quality of the service is declining as regulations force VRS providers to reduce costs by using fewer certified and experienced interpreters. [2]. With call volume as the driver for funding interpreters are required to make the relay call as quickly as possible. This establishes the interpreter as very strongly working in the conduit model of interpreting rather than in a more collaborative way. J. L Brunson describes it thus: "In this new method of service delivery interpreters are regulated in such a way to produce a non-person who acts as a go-between for the deaf and non-deaf person"

In Europe, where there are fewer, and generally smaller, VRS providers, services are often provided from a room with a single work station or from an interpreter's home office. The large call centre model has been broadly rejected citing issues of confidentiality amongst others. Interpreters typically work on VRS for three to four hours at a time and combine this with working in the community. This method of providing the service means that the interpreter lacks immediate access to support in the event of a difficult or lengthy call. There is less pressure to make a high volume of calls as services are funded differently therefore interpreters are able to take time preparing with the Deaf person prior to placing the relay call. In their study on turn organisation in video interpreting Warnicke and Plejert comment that "if the interpreter has a knowledge of what is the essence of a call...the interpreter is able to more readily anticipate which direction the interaction will take." 4.

At signvideo, the largest provider of VRS in the UK, services are provided both from single work stations and in small call centres. Those interpreters working on their own find that access to an instant messaging service or "chat' box is essential. It allows them to interact with colleagues based in the call centre or elsewhere and reduces the sense of isolation. In a profession that rarely has the opportunity to work with colleagues the sense of isolation can be magnified if the interpreter is based in a room on their own for a lengthy period of time. The small call centre gives instant access to support and interpreters working in this setting find it useful on a number of counts particularly when working on lengthy conference calls or with Deaf customers who may not be fluent in British Sign Language. Careful arrangement of the room and the use of sound absorbent wall coverings mean that over-lapping calls do not cause too much interference, although particularly loud-voiced interpreters sometimes have to be reminded to moderate their volume of speech. Signvideo's policy is that all interpreters working in the VRS service are registered and qualified with a minimum of three years working in the community. This is seen as essential to providing a high quality service to customers.

Making the Most of a Limited Resource

As stated in the introduction qualified sign language interpreters are a limited resource. Deaf people sometimes experience a delay in receiving services that hearing people can access more quickly simply because of the need to wait for an interpreter to be available. We all have heard the frustrating stories of Deaf people who attended an appointment and whose time was wasted because the service either neglected to, or was unable to, book an interpreter. As an interpreter it can be frustrating to find yourself booked all day to provide support for one individual only to find that they require your services for a fraction of the time when you are fully aware that there are other Deaf people who require an interpreter who are not getting a service. Whilst acknowledging that there are some settings where an on-site interpreter is a necessity, VRS can be a viable alternative particularly where the interpreter is required for a short period of time.

In July 2013 the average length of a call made through signvideo was just over 5 minutes in duration with 1 in 40 lasting longer than 30 minutes. Each interpreter processed an average of 520 calls during the month. The average time that a customer had to wait to access the services of an interpreter was less than 1 minute, a significant improvement on booking an on-site interpreter.

Case Studies

In this series of short case studies it is hoped to demonstrate that VRS is a useful supplement to on-site interpreters without being a replacement for such provision.

Case Study 1: CH, working in an IT support role, was told that she could not be promoted as the senior role required telephone contact with field engineers from time to time. Provision of VRS made promotion possible as it met the ad hoc need of phone calls in a cost effective way. On-site interpreters continue to be booked for team meetings, supervisions, appraisal and training

Case Study 2: AD is self-employed and was losing business as customers were calling his mobile phone and leaving messages that he was unable to hear. When advertising his services locally using text relay he found that customers were deterred from calling by having to enter a prefix number to access that service. Provision of VRS with a video messaging facility means that he can now access messages and respond, thus winning more work. He has found that having a direct dial number has increased the number of enquiries that he receives.

Case Study 3: CC works for a local council and needs to phone clients and equipment providers to make appointments and follow up on provision of equipment. Previously she had to rely on office administration staff to do this but she is now able to make these calls herself; using voice carry-over she speaks directly to her clients whilst the interpreter interprets their responses. Provision of VRS means that she is now independent and can work from home in the same way as her hearing colleagues.

Case Study 4: DH works for an international company where his colleagues are based across the country and internationally. Previously unable to access team and project meetings that took place via tele-conferencing he is now able to make a contribution. When project meetings are set up to respond to a fast-changing environment he is as well briefed on the situation as his hearing colleagues.

Case Study 5: HS is an interpreter with a young family who has found providing VRS from home has enabled her to continue to earn an income. Working from her home office she uses Google Chat to communicate with colleagues throughout her shift. Having a transfer facility on the interpreter interface allows her to share lengthy calls with colleagues. With the schedule arranged more than a month in advance she can coordinate her diary with her partner's thus minimising childcare costs.

Meeting the Needs of the Interpreter and the Deaf Community

Clearly VRS is still in its infancy and more work needs to be done in researching how this new area of provision can best meet the needs of all the stakeholders concerned. Stakeholders include not only the Deaf community and interpreters but also the hearing customers, telecoms companies and government, who may be called upon to fund or to legislate to ensure that the service is developed and made accessible to all members of the community who require the service. It is important that all these stakeholders meet around the table to discuss what each of them requires from VRS.

In the UK, ASLI (The Association of Sign Language Interpreters) has a working group focussing on VRS, giving a voice to the profession. Ukcod (United Kingdom Council on Deafness), an umbrella organisation of charities working with Deaf, Deafblind and Hard of Hearing people, runs Deaf Access Communication. Ofcom, acts as the industry regulator on behalf of the government and telecoms companies are not state-owned. Drawing these disparate groups together and balancing their sometimes competing needs continues to be a slow process.

Further work needs to be done in looking at how working in VRS affects interpreters' working practice as identified by Tracey Tyer in her MA thesis "Presence - as good as being there?" It is also incumbent on VRS providers to engage with their customers to ascertain that their needs are met and continue to be met as the service and the technology develops. What is evident is that as Brunson says "what was once thought of as a relationship between two people who do not share a language, and thus use the services of a third person must now be understood as a web of relationships that spans multiple locations and involves multiple actors who are not immediately present."

1. Www.interpretereducation.org/Specialization/vrs-vri
2. Www.streetleverage.com/2012/10/sign-language-interpreters-the-unintended-victims-of-vrs-regulation-change/
3. Studies in Interpretation Vol.8: Video Relay Services - Intricacies of Sign Language Access. J. L. Brunson. Pub GU Press
4. Journal of Pragmatics 44 (2012) 1313-1334: Turn-organisation in mediated phone interaction using Video Relay Service (VRS). C. Warnicke and C. Plejert
5. Call centre statistics reproduced by kind permission of signvideo.
6. Presence - as good as being there? T. Tyer 2011 unpublished.
7. Brunson op cit

Okan Kubus (Germany): Advantages and challenges of video relay sevices (VRS) in Germany: perspectives of vrc interpreters and deaf customers

Okan Kubus is a sign linguist, psycholinguist and a deaf sign language interpreter, phd student at the Universität Hamburg and works as a project leader for the German Society of the Hearing-Impaired - Support Groups and Professional Associations. He graduated in 2005 in Cognitive Sciences at the Informatics Institute, Middle East Technical University in Ankara, Turkey before starting his doctoral studies in Turkish Sign Language at the Universität Hamburg. He works as a freelance sign language interpreter for German Sign Language, Turkish Sign Language and International Signs after having passed his state examination in 2011. He is currently leading a project about the communication skills of deaf and hard of hearing individuals in interpreted video-relay conversations.

Contact details for correspondence: okankubus@gmail.com

Abstract: Advantages and Challenges of Video Relay Services in Germany: Perspectives of VRS Interpreters and Deaf Customers. The increasing use of Video Relay Services (VRS) in Germany, established since the early 2000s, has, without a doubt, been a huge step forward in the direction of facilitating communication without barriers, especially in occupational environments. However, some uncalled for issues have arisen, since interpreting in VRS strongly varies from face-to-face interpreting, which may not have been expected by interpreters and customers alike in the past. So far, no empirical studies have been done on this in Germany.

A questionnaire was designed to help gather understanding about the exact process of telephone interpreting and collecting the possible distracting factors as well as applicable solutions. It was answered by eleven interpreters working in Video Relay

Service companies such as Telesign and Tess. In order to add perspectives from the deaf customers of the named companies, eleven deaf participants have been interviewed.

While the results from both groups overlapped partly, there were also issues that appear to be perceived in very contradictory ways mainly due to difference in cultural protocols and the lack of knowledge on either side of the conversation. Similar observations have been made in related publications (Timm, 2000; Dickinson, 2002; Napier, Goswell & Mckee, 2006) and have also been observed in telephone-interpreted conversations with different spoken languages (Luke & Pavlidou, 2002). Thoughts on resulting implications for interpreter training and customer information though still need to be developed. It will be discussed how interpreters and institutions of sign language interpreting as well as the deaf community might deal with the raised issues to maximize the facility in telephone interpreting settings.

References

Dickinson, J. (2002). Telephone Interpreting—'Hello, is anyone there?'. Deaf Worlds: Inter- national Journal of Deaf Studies, 18 (2), pp. 34-38.

Luke, K. K. & Pavlidou, T. S. (2002). Studying telephone calls: beginnings, developments, perspectives. In: K.K. Luke & T. S. Pavlidou (Eds.) Telephone Calls. Unity and Diversity in Conversational Structure Across Languages and Cultures. John Benjamins Publishing Co., Amsterdam, pp. 3-21.

Napier, J.; mckee, R. & Goswell, D. (2006). Sign Language Interpreting theory and practice in Australia and New Zealand. The Federation Press.

Timm, D. (2000). Telephone interpreting. American Sign Language Interpreting Resources.

Http://asl_interpreting.tripod.com/situational_studies/dtl.htm.

ADVANTAGES and CHALLENGES of VIDEO RELAY SERVICES (VRS) in GERMANY
PERSPECTIVES of VRS INTERPRETERS and DEAF CUSTOMERS

Okan Kubus (German Society of the Hearing-Impaired - Support Groups and Professional Associations / Deutsche Gesellschaft der Hörgeschädigten - Selbsthilfe und Fachverbände e.V. & Universität Hamburg)

Motivation
- In VRS, some uncalled for issues have arisen, since interpreting in VRS strongly varies from face-to-face interpreting (Limbach et al, 2012), which may not have been expected by interpreters and costumers alike in the past.
- So far, no empirical studies have been done on this in Germany.

GOALS:
- Raising awareness on telephone etiquette among deaf and hard of hearing individuals
- Observation of telephone interpreting, discovering the dynamics of conversational dialogue among VRS users, hearing interlocutors and interpreters

Background
- Telephoning is a relatively new communication form for the Deaf Community. (Dickinson, 2003, 260)
- Telephone interpreting is a highly complex task, and one may have reasons for claiming that it is among the most complicated areas that any interpreter working between signed and spoken languages may face.
- Although it (telephone interpreting) seems a simple task, interpreting telephone calls can be very challenging depending on the purpose and content of the call and because telephone use is based on hearing cultural protocols (Napier et al. 2006, 138)
- There is no updated written material on telephone interpreting (worldwide) (Timm, 2000).

METHODOLOGY

Survey / Interview Design
- A survey was designed to help gather understanding about the exact process of telephone interpreting and collecting the possible distracting factors as well as applicable solutions. The survey includes metadata questions and open ended questions grouped into 9 subcategories.
- Hearing interlocutors and sign language interpreters answered the survey in written form. The VRS users were interviewed via webcam and were asked the same questions as in the survey.

Participants
	#	%
VRS users (U)	12/215	5.6 %
VRS interpreters (I)	11/49	22.4 %
Hearing interlocutors (H)	5	

FINDINGS

Pre-information before telephone conversation needed? (U)
- 7/12 deaf informants do not see this as a must. Giving the interpreter the needed contact details is seen as sufficient.
- 2/12 deaf informants do not like to be asked questions before a conversation. One of the reasons: The connection is chargeable immediately after calling the interpreter.

(I) - All interpreters: Pre-information given before a real telephone conversational is considered very much desirable. It does not have to be long: Name, numbers, way to address the person, previous knowledge of the interlocutor about VRS services and terminology to be used during the conversation, if available, would suffice.

Background knowledge of the interlocutors?
(U) - Knowledge of telephone etiquette (self-assessment of deaf users: 8=good, 3=adequate, 1=not sure (out of 12).
(I) - All interpreters think deaf users generally lack the required background information regarding telephone etiquette, i.e. dealing with different degrees of formality, hotlines, call centers, mailboxes, making the decision why and when to call and how to go about the conversation.
(H) - All hearing interlocutors think their hearing-impaired conversation partners have enough background information on telephone etiquette.

Decision-making in a telephone conversation (interpreters)?
(I) - 10/11 of the interpreters think decision-making plays an important role in telephone interpreting. Since they form a cultural bridge, they sometimes feel the need to adapt the conversation in a way that is more suitable for hearing people.

Technical requirements?
(U) - Some deaf informants find the technical requirements for the use of telephone interpreting services to be challenging.
(I) - Sometimes technical problems occur and the call has to be ended abruptly. Most of the users do not have ideal technical equipment.

Satisfied with the overall flow of telephone conversations?
(U) - 3/12 deaf informants feel unsure about when to end the conversation, one declared that she/he tended to wait for a signal from the interpreter.
(I) - Interpreters said that some calls, some calls do not start and end in a way that is typical for telephone conversations. Sometimes calls are ended by the deaf users even though the hearing interlocutor is not finished.
(H) - Most challenging parts in using this service: Receiving the first call (irritation due to lack of experience) and coping with pauses during the conversation. Some hearing interlocutors with more experience develop strategies like having patience, speaking slowly and clearly, etc.

Linguistic aspects?
(I) - The deaf informants said that some interpreters have difficulty understanding fingerspelled words and special terminology related to the users' work environment.
- One informant thinks that some interpreters fail in finding a suitable register/style choice for her/him.
- One informant thinks that she/he feels better when signing slowly for the interpreter.
- The users have difficulties understanding when the interpreters:
  - do not use clear nonmanual means and expressions
  - sign hastily or use a narrow signing space
  - do not use clear mouthing since there are various dialectal variations in DGS

According to the interpreters:
- Since telephone interpreting (2-dimensional) is very different from face-to-face interpreting and also, some technical problems may arise during a call, it is very challenging to gather understandable signing from the TeSign/Telesign users.
- Challenges: Different degrees of competency of the users, many signs specific to regional variation, finding a suitable register/style, use of specific terminology, not possible to be prepared by seeing a document that will be discussed during the conversation

Adequate set-up quality?
(U) - All deaf informants think the quality of the interpreters' set-up is fairly professional

(I) Interpreters report experience with:
- Poor lighting quality (100 %)
- Locating the camera in front of a window or a door (100 %)
- No adequate focus and positioning of the camera (82 %)
- Low camera quality (73 %)
- More than one person in front of the camera (64 %)
- Clothes not ideal (73 %)
- Distractions in the user's background (91 %)
- others: The user eats (18%), uses only one hand when signing (18%), signs to another person during the call (9%)

(H) - The hearing informants think the services are useful and effective. Some of them emphasized the services ease the communication between hearing and hearing-impaired individuals.

(Self-)Judgment of users and need of further training?
(U) - 9/12 deaf users would like to join workshops or seminars regarding the use of VRS services, but only if there are interpreters involved as well and the training is practice-oriented.
(I) - All interpreters think the TeSign/Telesign users have to attend an introductory training regarding telephone etiquette. It is considered to be necessary to prepare material for that purpose.

(Self-)Judgment of interpreters' competence and need of further training?
(U) - All deaf users think the interpreters need to attend regular training opportunities to further their competence regarding terminology, doing voice-over, different regional dialects and managing appropriate closeness and distance.
(I) - 7/11 interpreters think they need further training themselves: learning to deal with difficult calls, practising different regional variations, doing voice-over and improving their rhetoric skills.

DISCUSSION

- The differences in replies when it comes to what is and is not part of the interpreter's task indicates a need for further investigation, exchange of ideas and training on the issue. The degree as to how much telephone interpreting varies from face-to-face interpreting is not to be underestimated. New technologies are not only a means to ease communication, they are just as well challenges and spark a difficult, but rewarding dialogue.

- Immense heterogeneity of the group of deaf users of VRS interpreting → how can deaf individuals who have not had experience with telephone conversations gain knowledge on the non-written telephone protocols of hearing people?
  - Workshops, raising awareness in VRS Users → need for training materials on these issues
  - (or) Let them "learn by doing"?

References
Dickinson, J. (2003): Telephone Interpreting—Hello, is anyone there? Deaf Worlds. Intn. national Journal of Deaf Studies, 19 (2), pp. 34-50.
Limbach, A., Ruppert, H., Schulte, C. & Hangemann R. (2012): Beruftsbild DrolgY durch Technik- und Fernsdolmetscher? – Bericht über eine Fachtagung aus Anlass des 10-jährigen Bestehens der Telesign Deutschland GmbH. Das Zeichen 27(90), pp. 144-153.
Napier, J., McKee, R. & Goswell, D. (2006): Sign Language Interpreting: theory and practice in Australia and New Zealand. The Federation Press.
Timm, D. (2000): Telephone Interpreting. American Sign Language Interpreting Resources: http://asl_interpreting.tripod.com/industry_studies/dt.htm
efsli conference 2013 – 13th – 15th September 2013
Ljubljana, Slovenia

Email: okankubus@gmail.com

The project is funded by:

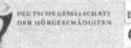

Bundesministerium für Arbeit und Soziales

Tracey Tyler (UK): Don't leave me hanging on the telephone...

Tracey Tyler: I am an interpreter with 13 years experience, particularly in the areas of theatre, deaf-blind, haptic communication and video remote interpreting (VRI). I am a member of the ASLI VRS working group investigating the impact of VRI on the UK interpreting profession and I also work as a home-based remote interpreter. I graduated from the EUMASLI programme with a specialist area of research in VRI interaction, completing a study of professional isolation in VRI. My thesis explored how presence was experienced by VRI interpreters. My future research will be a comparative analysis of stress factors in remote and call centre VRI interpreters.

Contact details for correspondence: info@colecomms.com

Abstract: Human beings are social animals with a fundamental need to belong. Our relationships 'subtly embrace us in the warmth of self-affirmation, the whispers of encouragement, and the meaningfulness of belonging' (Hughes et al, 2004). This factor of belonging emerges as one of the most important issues to be explored in relation to remote employment. This is no less true in the interpreting discipline. As Moser-Mercer has suggested (2003) remote interpreting should 'be subjected to careful analysis as regards its impact on the physical and psychological well-being of the interpreter'. Advances in digital technologies have enabled work activities to be distributed among employees in remote locations as 'telecommuting' (Gajendran & Harrison, 2007).

efsli 2013 proceedings

www.ingramcontent.com/pod-product-compliance
Lightning Source LLC
Chambersburg PA
CBHW052101230426
43662CB00036B/1751